A MADDENING DISREGARD FOR THE PASSAGE OF TIME

Other books by the author

POETRY
Dawn Visions
Burnt Heart/Ode to the War Dead
This Body of Black Light Gone Through the Diamond
The Desert is the Only Way Out
The Chronicles of Akhira
The Blind Beekeeper
Mars & Beyond
Laughing Buddha Weeping Sufi
Salt Prayers
Ramadan Sonnets
Psalms for the Brokenhearted
I Imagine a Lion
Coattails of the Saint
Abdallah Jones and the Disappearing-Dust Caper
Love is a Letter Burning in a High Wind
The Flame of Transformation Turns to Light
Underwater Galaxies
The Music Space
Cooked Oranges
Through Rose Colored Glasses
Like When You Wave at a Train and the Train Hoots Back at You
In the Realm of Neither
The Fire Eater's Lunchbreak
Millennial Prognostications
You Open a Door and it's a Starry Night
Where Death Goes
Shaking the Quicksilver Pool
The Perfect Orchestra
Sparrow on the Prophet's Tomb
A Maddening Disregard for the Passage of Time

THEATER / THE FLOATING LOTUS MAGIC OPERA COMPANY
The Walls Are Running Blood
Bliss Apocalypse

PROSE
Zen Rock Gardening
The Little Book of Zen
Zen Wisdom

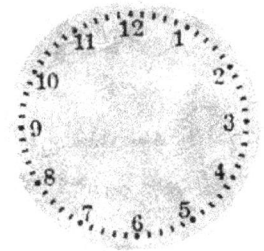

A MADDENING DISREGARD FOR THE PASSAGE OF TIME

poems

November 17, 1989 – May 20, 1990

Daniel Abdal-Hayy Moore

The Ecstatic Exchange
2009
Philadelphia

A Maddening Disregard for the Passage of Time
Copyright © 2009 Daniel Abdal-Hayy Moore
All rights reserved.
Printed in the United States of America

For quotes any longer than those for critical articles and reviews, contact:
The Ecstatic Exchange,
6470 Morris Park Road, Philadelphia, PA 19151-2403
email: abdalhayy@danielmoorepoetry.com

First Edition
ISBN: 978-0-578-04677-8
Published by The Ecstatic Exchange,
6470 Morris Park Road, Philadelphia, PA 19151-2403

Also available from The Ecstatic Exchange:
Knocking from Inside, poems by Tiel Aisha Ansari

Cover collage by the author
Book Design: Ian Whiteman; Realization: the author
Back cover photograph taken in Marrakech, Morocco, at the Sidi Shikr Conference, 2009

DEDICATION

To

Shaykh ibn al-Habib

(and the continuation of the Habibiyya)

Shaykh Bawa Muhaiyuddeen,

all shuyukh of instruction and ma'arifa,

and

Baji Tayyaba Khanum

of the unsounded depths

And to those who turn away from the world to The Real, Who does not die, and have, in the world's eyes at least, *a maddening disregard for the passage of time...*

---

*The earth is not bereft
of Light*

CONTENTS

A Word About the Title   10
Self-Effacement in Witnessing the Essence
    by Shaykh Muhammad ibn al-Habib   12
In the End   15
Giant Head   16
Ferns   18
An Insolubly Tall Building   20
Bodies of Women, Bodies of Men   21
Climb a Stairway   22
Hindlegs   23
The House of Tigers   24
Oaks   28
The Circular Garden   31
Sky House on Ozone Hill   37
The Wild Stars   41
Leaf   43
Night & Day   45
Circular Stairways   46
Each New Poem   49
Noise in the Kitchen   51
Natural Monuments   58
Tyrants Drive Past Statues of Themselves   60
The Mysterious Door   61
Presumption   64
When Friends Come to Visit   65
When We Look Up at the Stars   67
Time to Sing of Love   70
If We Entered a World   72
Elephant Tusks   74

Everything's Alive   76
Seated at the Piano   78
The Garden in the Pupil   81
I Was Given a Box   82
God's Face   84
Three Days, Three Wishes   85
The Night Floats   92
Eyes Plants   95
Music   98
Our House is Flexible Enough   102
In a World with No Time for Poetry   105
Fifteen Minutes to Write This   107
Up a Ramp into the Fuselage   112
The Imagined Landscape   115
You Are What You Eat   123
Child in Pain   125
Time-Drought   128
The Cup That Records the Event   132
When You Become Naked   136
Language is a Door   139
Scarf of Sweet Visions   142
People at a Poetry Reading   147
A Vehicle for the Expeditionary Imagination   153
Circus Vargas   158
Exists!   165
A Maddening Disregard for the Passage of Time   167
Spring Ruminations   169
I'm Struck by the Desire   176
Some of the Mysteries of the Self   183
Transformations   197
Bad Dream   200

The Eyes   202
Landscapes Come in Different Sizes   206
Ice-Swans   208
Cut a Tree   210
Theme and Variation   211
Will We Have to Invent Our Own Forest of Trees   214
Why Does the Soul Love Poetry   218
Where Does It All Come From   221
Swirl   225
Beetles   228
The Deepest Ground   229
House fronts   231
First Teacher, Last Teacher   238
Time   240

A WORD ABOUT THE TITLE

Although this has been the working title from the inception of this series of poems, only now do I see a facet of it that has only been sublimated (now *sublimed?*) until now. I'm reminded of William Blake's adage, *"Eternity is in love with the productions of Time."* And I'm struck by how Blake himself, absorbed as he was in Eternity, was thought mad by the people of the world who were not so similarly absorbed. He didn't care. He worked on with blithe energy and fierce determination. And it is this aspect of the title that intrigues me, and that really informed the ongoing inspiration of these poems.

While we are born into time, and at death we slide out of time altogether into whatever space we might theologically or anti-theologically conceive (eternity, nothingness?), in a supreme moment we might taste timelessness, fleeting though it may be (though that fleetingness too still exists as a component of time).

A nice, practical, everyday disregard for time might be an enviable position to take, if we have such luxury in our hectic full-speed ahead culture. Hobos and saints seem to be nonchalant about it. Walt Whitman says *"I lean and loafe at my ease, observing a spear of summer grass."* And butterflies flutter beautifully perhaps unaware of their fleetingness. Can disregard, alone, then, abolish time? Not if someone is waiting for us at the door to hurry and put our coat on.

Which is the "timeless" (or at least spontaneous) moment from which this title originally came: my dear wife Malika, waiting for me, with a little spark of impatience, said, *"You have a maddening disregard for the passage of time!"* And in reply I said, *"What a great title for a book of poems!"* That's how we are. That's how I am.

But a consideration of timelessness is something far more profound and worthy of both contemplation and our wisdom-heart's constant emulation. It seems to confound as well as inspire mathematicians, as well as mathematically challenged poets, down the timeless ages. Many of the poems in this book have time as a theme, or as a kind of subtext, though as is usual with me for the most part, a "received" book title for an ensuing, chronological writing of poems gives a kind of loose trellis for the chunk of "time" proceeding from it in which the poems flow into composition and grow into a collection, without any planned, rational premeditation.

But how might these poems finally be classified? Are they Sufi poems, in either the usual sense, or in a rather novel sense after all, which takes into account American poetry from Ezra Pound through the Beat or San Francisco Renaissance period (including some non-Beat poets, such as Robert Duncan), since I am grounded in Islamic Sufism and it pulsates I believe quite "aurally" and "orally" through all my work? But in the case of this book and its title, if it's a "disregarding" of time, do I betray the famous tradition of the Prophet Muhammad, peace be upon him, which also serves as the epigraph of the final poem of this book: *"Do not curse time, for time is Allah"*? A wonderfully imponderable Koan of spiritual Presence! And is the answer to it some representation of the Eternal Moment? *"Eternity is in love with the productions of time..."*

Additionally, I would note the inclusion, in a version of mine based on translations directly from the Arabic, of a poem (the two pages following) from his *diwan* of poem-songs, which is sung by his disciples and seekers across the world, of my first Sufi shaykh, the majestic and perfect man of Allah, Shaykh Muhammad ibn al-Habib of Fez, may Allah be pleased with him, buried in the sweet garden of his tomb in Meknes, Morocco, since 1972. His Light, from the ocean of the Prophet, is what spreads throughout time and space. He (and all great friends of God, living and in the Unseen) was a serene exemplar of Time and Eternity's divine blend.

SELF-EFFACEMENT IN WITNESSING THE ESSENCE

My Beloved's Face appeared to me
and shone in the hour before dawn.

Its light enveloped my heart,
and I prostrated — my soul shattered.

He said: Arise and ask of Me!
Whatever you desire is yours.

I replied: *You! You* are all I need!
I can't live a moment without You!

He said: My servant, glad tidings are yours.
Take comfort in the vision you've been given!

You are a treasure stored up for My servants.
You stand as a reminder for humanity.

Know that all goodness and beauty in souls
spreads forth from Me.

Though the attributes of My Essence are inwardly hidden
they are mirrored in the world's shadowy traces.

The reality of the universe is spiritual meanings
projected in the images of outward forms.

All those who grasp this subtle allusion
are people graced by discerning wisdom,

while no one who stays apart from us
can taste life's true sweetness.

Our Lord, bless Muhammad the praised one
whose light envelops humanity.

— *from the Diwan of Shaykh Muhammad ibn al-Habib*

(This version revised from the translation by Aisha Tarjuman Bewley, with inestimable help from Abdarrahman Fitzgerald and Shakir Masoud)

I want to sing like birds sing
not worrying who hears
or what they think.

    — *Rumi*

a beetle recognizes you,
you are about
to happen,
grubs
spin around you,

the Great
Sphere
permits your passage

    — *Paul Celan*

IN THE END

In the end to go your own way completely
disregarding completely what you think your
literary hero would think and then try to
think the same way, do a whole new thing
completely, starting and
ending with bare bones. Not to

imagine feverish nightmares or gloriously fleeting
beauties like a gush of light in the shape of a
fiery tunnel lined in mother-of pearl
behind a giant leering head of a faun at the
end of a decadent decade just because you think
Rimbaud would have liked it — he ended up
more concerned with the price of
tradable merchandise anyway —

We are suspended on earth for a tiny space.
Our feet hardly touch ground before we are
snatched away. The more we

live the more the pattern fills out,
fragments come together and fit or sit
lopsidedly jostled together, but something gets
fleshed out in fuller dimensions the more we just

let things show us their wandering ways.

GIANT HEAD

It's a giant head suspended above the marsh
   casting a strange light against the hill,
its outlines run like water, its eyes zoom forward
looking for sights, it's an elegant almost
   classical head, elements inside its
contours are at war.

It stands in the air there still enough for me to see.
For example, the sensual
lips are in perfect repose, you expect
true and resonant words to jolt out, chipping
   unscalable canyons in the air.
Horse heads emerge from its cheeks.
Its features are aflame with unearthly passions.
A door in its forehead
lets down stairways.
Its ears are curled abalone hoops, ships'
   horns blow out of them at
     great haunted distances across the sea.
Rippling shadows fall below its hair.
Street-scenes of megalopolis flicker along its chin.
Clouds shift across its hairline. Flames
   chase them. Curved eyes look out with a
     great yellow light.
The landscape is crisp where its
   terrible gaze has landed.
It can't turn its gaze away. It looks

down at you forever.

Well, not forever, only
as long as this moment lasts in the
test-tube that shoots up and down past the
earth's dimensions out of time.

Then its eyes flicker. It looks at seas of blood
pulsing around our feet. We are

standing on a steep hillside watching this head
hover here, looking at us, waiting for the
first move.

It's a giant head suspended above the marsh.

FERNS

He wanted so much to be involved in the
   unfurling of ferns that he
      became a fern,
fuzzy with golden fringe at the
   edges, climbing
      house fronts. He saw the

entire universe as fern-like, the coming-to-birth of that
baby's clenched fist at the
tips of baby ferns.

Windows of light opened in the fern's spores.
Ferns tangled up through branches of thicker
   mature growths, the ones with
   latin names, histories, plotted destinations.
The ones that banged against
      house fronts, left deep
         scratches raw as
wounded flesh. The

soft ferns softened the blows of the
harsher realities, lending a
   veil of green light from other worlds to the
compound, manufactured
      hard edges of this one.
The fern wanted to encompass everything in its
   uncurling embrace, surround everything in its love,

but remain always

in a state of coming-to-birth, a
baby's tiny

soft clenched fists at the
glowing tender tips of

baby ferns.

11/17

AN INSOLUBLY TALL BUILDING

An insolubly
   tall building, a life.

You enter one of its rooms and get to
  know it, then you have to
    move.

In another room you are faced with a
   host of enigmas:
How to make a
  living, how to raise your
    kids.

Daily existence looms tall.

BODIES OF WOMEN, BODIES OF MEN

Bodies of women open like
   underground entrances to
      valuable territories.

Bodies of men pulse to a single
sharp point like above-ground
     detonations.

Joined, iguanas swerve their gazes,
    monarch butterflies
       gather on trees,
   stones in rivers
       glisten.

                                            11/21

CLIMB A STAIRWAY

Climb a stairway that is
   humpback whale backs
out to the middle of the
   ocean and back.

Climb out a window that is
blinking owl's eyes on a
   high branch, then come back.

Swerve and curl on the bared heart of the
   earth like a serpent fresh from its
     egg covered in black.

Bob like a spring in a wind on the
rim of your nest with
equally green fledglings having an anxiety attack, then

flop out in total confusion to find

you are flying!

                                            11/27

HINDLEGS

Hindlegs of jackrabbits scissoring through tall grass,
hindlegs of giraffes taller than the grass,
gorgeous human hindlegs on a
   giant woman-creature whose
      hair is as
         tall as Victoria Falls,
shapely flesh-tones glistening like
  ivory in late
     African sun,

hindlegs of kangaroos which are
   almost all hindleg, they
      crouch down to
         drink nearly
folding entirely in two,

hindlegs God has
   given us to
      spring up in the air, for
joy, for safety, for
   basketball, for pure
      springiness, these

levers and pulleys, planks and roller-ball
   feet that get us
     up and moving, striding

long along the tall grass, standing
tall in the

long grass on our

own hindlegs!

$\hspace{20em}$ 11/30

THE HOUSE OF TIGERS

There's a
 house on a
  ledge overlooking
deep canyons and
 majestic things
   go on inside
    of it,
 a
tiger couple
 lives there in
pale flannel suits, they
 stand on their
  hindlegs and look
 noble and
  fresh, pointy ears
alert, noses
 twitching, eyes
 bright.

They are
domesticated
 tigers with
 first names and
  dietary
preferences, they
sit on
 couches and
love to gaze
 out at the

canyons. Great
predatory
  birds
  cast
    shadows on the
canyon walls opposite in the
  light of the
    late
      afternoon,
circle and
  circle in the
open space before
    diving, and the tigers
just
  love to
watch their
    sleek
performances.

Sunlight in the
  tigers' den: Golden
stripes on
    raffia
furniture. Tigers of

elegance extending their
  paws on
long glass
    tabletops. Luxurious tigers of
languor
    stretching

out for late
afternoon siestas. Tigers of

  admirable
    control and
  wisdom looking
seriously concerned over
    coffee at our

sweet
  human
    confusions.

                                                11/30

OAKS

Oak trees throw their branches around like
   ladies shaking out their hair.

They stand above ground like arthritic claws which
look like they were clenching the soil,
but are now upturned to
   clench, instead, the air. They are

grandiose in profusion, serrated leaves like so many
punctuation marks or the scatterbrained sequins of the
   starry heavens, rattling in their

silences, stretching their
jagged edges into the
   sky for
     blue jays to squawk in.

Oaks are like faithful nannies, not superficially
glamorous in themselves, not like those
glossy Cecil Beaton photographs of Greta Garbo looking
   skyward, head thrown back in ecstatic
     exquisiteness, but plain and
loyal, mottled
bark, gray-silver and thick in scabby chunks, crabbed
trunks, gnarly
branches, something distinctly
Germanic about them, whereas they are actually as
   rugged and
     seedy as the

weatherbeaten California indians themselves must have been
sitting around the bases of oaks, grinding
    acorns.

Born in Oakland, adolescence spent in
oak-filled canyons, a buddy and I built a
tree-house and two-story fort in a
clump of oaks, getting their

sap on our fingers after driving ignorant nails into them,
the flesh wound of red inner tree flesh, the
  musky, acrid smell of oak sap, then

the lovely creaking of wind through their scabrous branches
when we
lay in our sleeping bags inside the
fort we'd built, deep inside the
bodies of the sheltering oaks
to sleep, two satisfied master-builders,
enwrapped in the sound of their
deeper snores.

Ants love to thread through the natural trail-blazed
gaps in their bark.

Oaks are associated with darting
  birds.

Hills often have an oak or two like
  snarling red setters
guarding the hillside. Oaks

flourish on the

hillside of a

grown-up heart.

                                        12/3

THE CIRCULAR GARDEN
an active/static tapestry

A hundred ladders leaned up against a continuous rosy wall
under a sky like an overturned black cube
inside a high-walled circular courtyard with tiny shell-shaped
pool in the center and stylized
Renaissance rose-bushes growing in neat borders along the wall
at night artificially lit by flashes of distant fireworks
promising ultimate and ardently
   longed-for escape or

showing instead a kind of

spa people needing solace might climb down into
to spend their few remaining years or decades
speaking in perfect sentences, drawing geometrical
mazes, plucking polished lutes.

Speaking perfect sentences. Flicking their eyes at each other and
communicating with
 precision and beauty. Actually
appreciating the beauty of the communication while also
taking in the meaning, the
   "thing communicated" for use and cognition.
Everything in its place. Not
heavily categorized, nor metallically
   assembled for further reference, those eye-flicks not
mechanical, but metrical, rhythmic
recognitions of self-assurance and concentration with
artless openness to an outside world worth

    taking in. Small

creatures also walk at our feet, some of them
cats, slinking occasionally around our
ankles, or sitting nearby for aloof
  petting, or even
    coming onto our laps for that
subtle electric link to the heartbeat of creatureness,
non-human, linked almost as much with
wild animals as with
  us. But then there are
other beasts (for they must be called

beasts) nosing about the green, such as
pointy-nosed, peach-colored, smooth, beady-eyed snufflers
that keep their snouts on the ground while emitting
huffing sounds, not
  abrasive, but gentle
    huffing sounds, a
  contrapuntal background to either the
lilting melodies of the lutes, the soft
    transfer of language-nodes, or the
silent stroking of
  silver-haired cats. The night wears

on. Night-birds also come
  into the picture. Truly
marvellous multi-colored tropical variety. Birds of
Paradise displaying their
  visually fragrant
    plumage, flagrantly

    arrayed in great
golden curves and splashes of
   orange and red
    arcs of sudden
color against the darker, grayer
  foliage of the trees or against the
    blank rock surface of the
     walls.

There are also
 small birds like brownish
   knots in a
tapestry, details in the
    weave, they
weave in and out of the
  bushes and
    branches. We sit
watching them, or they just
  fly into and
   out of what we happen to be
watching, as we
  talk to each other, or
   walk arm in arm through the paths, going slowly
    across fields and sudden
yellow openings of meadow and distant
  farmland, smoke-curls from distant
    villages seen like
   pipe-smoke down a
     sloping hill, or against

against what I was going to say were

windows of dank factories, cold moist
   metal parts and gigantic
      wheels reaching from cold cement
floors veined with tiny capillaries of human blood to
distant cranial reaches of interior ceiling into which
wheel-curves hump like dunes in a desert at night,
the foreign sound of a horse neighing, the
   whinny of a restive
      horse just outside the garden wall, but also
the sound of a thriving and exciting
civilization with loud-speakers blasting
high-pitched popular songs in voices as
   excitable as interior
      bodily organs to an
         electric prod,

while inside the circular walls where a hundred
ladders are leaned
up against the
   walls there are also people who want to
escape, who see through eyes of hurt and hatred,
or at least see that the world inside these
walls is too
   small for them, for
     one reason or
another. They may be
   malcontents. They might be
     inspired and see with an
eyesight that beams past the normal
     irregularities of hard
        matter into areas

difficult to describe, which die
unsung in the persons of some, or are

articulated in rare forms by those who can
speak but whose language takes a long time to
learn. For them the hundred ladders spell
    escape. Escape for them means going
          anywhere out of
where they are. They may

pass the ones climbing down as they climb up
and out, they may feel sorry for the
deluded ones with lunar-lidded eyes and
   shy smiles climbing
     down those
hundred ladders into the
    garden, laugh
      harsh laughters in their
        hearts as they pass, thinking
"damned fools" while they are
   showing the way out to all
     mankind by the simple act of

hand over hand, rung by rung, foot first on the
first rung then
lifted to the next. Their

eyes don't really meet, they are
   vaguely aware of each other, really, the
ones climbing up and out
     too actually determined in their

bones to be off, the others so

contentedly descending into
    perfection, amazed anyone would
ever want to leave
sweet briar and hedge.

For a moment their
faces glow together, become
a single face smooth as porcelain, then
separate faces again, some rising
up and some climbing
carefully down, the flying twine of

swift wrens wrapping and
   unwrapping around them

both as they pass each other, darting
  noisily into
    thatch and verdant

foliage of tree and bush, of noise and
  hush, of the
    slow rush of

the inevitability
of it all.

                                      12/5

SKY HOUSE ON OZONE HILL

On a hill of sky sits a house of sky whose
　walls are both inside and outside,
doors are both
　　within and without, so that when you
go in one way you
come right out another, or if you
go to leave the
interior you swiftly
enter the exterior. What's

uncanny about this house is that we don't really
live here, nothing really
lives here, we leave
traces, oily rubbings on the
　walls, broken
　　fixtures, sashes that
　　　don't work, stuck
windows, sagging
　fences, but everything
　　goes with us when we
go, the

personal style that could
　　suddenly be
opposite depending on the
　new resident, so all your
plain mid-western paraphernalia of
　worn levis, transistor-radios, plastic spatulas and
　　country calendars are like a

vacant stare on the face of someone
just waking up for a
     moment until the

deposed Cambodian emperor moves in and suddenly
there are gilded knobs on the sofas, everything has
doilies, the kitchen smells of
   ginger and sesame oil, the
     bathroom has a
       golden tub on ivory legs with
sculpted claws. Nothing is the

same because
  nothing remains, our
     precious atomic
       shadows
slink swiftly along the alleyways of mortality's night
to escape into the greater blankness where
    slow xylophones play somber
       notes echoed back
          transformed into
sweet, thin music.

House of sky. Rooms of pure
atmosphere. Floors even
   shifting beneath us. Windows almost look out on things that
almost look real. Sound real. Assume

sensible spatial depth. But folks,

depth is elsewhere. You have to climb down

raw pink rock-slides into throbbing granite
canyons at the
   end of the yawn that seems to be
     space, into chambers of

jumbled dimensions, X-dimensions sitting through each other's
edges to give you a
    foothold, definite
mountain-lions passing regally along the
   just-glimpsed horizon, black
rainbows out of their eyes, or rather

it can't be described, every possible
description is too harshly architectural, even
   atomic structures with their
     maddening rationality and their
       sudden whims just to
   perplex us
are too satisfactorily geometrical, whereas

a long dark drop down a slow slope,
a passionately smooth coolness as if we could
   unfold our own selves out
     infinitely to unfold after
       unfold to where

funnels of starlight accommodate the
inner spaces, wedges of
   galaxy fit within the
     unfolds, and all of this

assumes our simple human dimension with our
very own silly human faces sitting right on our
neck-stalks like glistening innocent
   heads of elegant snails.

Unassuming smiles camouflage the total adventure.

Stairways cut out of
   rock crystal in the
painful stitches in our
    sides to secret

ascensions denote
more than language can,

the unself-conscious gesture of helplessness, total

submission to God's

greater rush.

                                            12/8

THE WILD STARS

Every person on earth
walks their entire life back and forth
   underneath the stars, but it seems as if
some never look up.

Babies crane their necks when they notice for the
   first time the
     ceiling's been replaced by
sprinkling lights of heavens, hot white pinpoints
beaming down through the sieve of
   dark in titillating dots. Things with

wings of various
   sizes and velocities pass
     by under its
concave canopy. Lions pounce on gazelles and
   quietly gnaw fresh flesh by moonlight under
     the fierce intensity of the night sky.

Hut-smoke curls gray snakes of fuzziness in
tiny wriggling threads up into the sparkling blanket of
the sky as it
   curves entirely
  around the globe.

A speck of three-masted boat in the moonlit sheen of open sea
has within it, the size of
   microbes, intelligent mites looking out through
telescopes and calculating with

     astrolabes in order to reach
        shore on schedule. The stars, the

silent stars are their counsellors.

A bead of water on marble, imperfectly
  round, heavier at the
    bottom, actually reflects
all the visible heavens and all the visible
    stars on the
  surface of its sides without any
    visible effort, even
 catching their progress from
   horizon to
   horizon before
evaporating un-immortally away.

On the blackened circular
surface of the
coffee in your coffee cup many of the
same stars are
    mirrored. You drink their
light with your last
  satisfied gulp.

Why do you hide the stars inside you?
The wild stars.

Why do you turn down their light?

                                              12/9

LEAF

A leaf opens and you're
   in Peru, walking through a
     ferny glade. A
rosebud opens and you're hanging from a
    thread of intricate Viennese conver-
       sation over
     porcelain tea. A leaf

drops and we're on a lonely English road at the
end of Fall, past rural houses with tall roofs of
   actual thatch. A

rose drifts brown petals to the
ground and the golden era of Spain's
   great caliphate of
     intellectual music browns like an old

photograph. The cast of
  characters dies. Wooden
    doors hang
slack on thin hinges.

A leaf opens on its
   branch or in your
hand, it takes on a
   life of its own. If you
lean real
   close you hear
choirs. A

leaf opens and you're in
heaven, a green place, a green so

rich and deep it has an odor to it,

a green that
  bathes itself along
    your inner stem.

                                                12/10

NIGHT & DAY

Night comes. One eyelid
   covers all.

Day comes. One eyelid
   opens.

Oh, of course, cars go around at night
   with their headlights on.

Some people die by day.

CIRCULAR STAIRWAYS

Circular stairways, circular gardens, circular
lives... *my God, how*
  desperately isolated most lives seem!

You take someone off the street and
sit them in front of a video camera to
talk for three minutes about love

and out come litanies of lonely pain and hopelessness,
no wild or sculpted trees where
rare three-crested golden birds of mysterious
longings perch, few
waterfalls whose glistening light shines so
brightly you
  have to wince or
    squint to see the
   outlines of desire's spiritual cascades, so few

natural landscapes, so few
daring adventures, so many

sobbing holes and nowhere to
clutch onto, only
places to fall from, so few
places to land! What have we

done to ourselves? Children forever, we seem to
want to
open large doors, but open

   the small one in the
middle with the
     full-length mirror on it
      instead.
Narcissus bends and
  kisses his lips while the
     mirror steams.

We seem to want to ride fleet white horses who
glide through sea-surf, but end up

walking wounded, tattered, barely bandaged instead.

Linked together, each segment of lives taken at
random from a random
  segment of population results in a

long drawn out cry for help only
vaguely perceived by the criers.

Behind the eyes of so few smolder
passionate fires, behind the
  eyes of so few extend long blue

lakes of happy serenity across which human sight skims
forward to look out
compassionate eyes.

Over and over again come the tensely enunciated words
"pain" and *"confusion"!* From
good looking women, from handsome men!

You could turn them all into
wood and the
world wouldn't
  miss their
    sound. The forest would

take them in its arms again
unformed, bruised
  saplings still, staring

dazed, dumb.

                                                   12/14

(Note: My wife and daughter and I participated in a video art-project called "The Love Tapes." In a little room off the street, where the artist had set up a video camera which she then left running, people off the street talked about love for three minutes, then each unedited segment was added to an oral history of peoples' views about love in America, 1989. My wife talked extemporaneously about love of God, I read a poem (City of Love) and my 8 year old daughter talked about all the things she loves best, her brother, her toys, her hamster, etc.)

EACH NEW POEM

With each new poem it's like there was never
any one before it that made
   any sense at all.

Naked and stupid, I grab a pen and let it
wriggle under my grasp. It
writes what it wants to.

I want colossal oceans at night, ocean-liners with
rows of cabin-lights under huge thunderheads
massed just before collision. Slate blue darkness.
Gigantic slosh of waves. Distant

tiny human cries in
implacable night.

And so it is. The pen just
wrote it out.

Anything else?

I want dense tropics, smell so
strong you
nearly swoon, so deeply
sweet, thick with
steam, colors so
rich your
heart can hardly
stand it. You

sink. The whole
world closes above
you with its
whistling tangles of flying
   toucans and
 glimpses of
   pale blue sky through the
nearly black mesh of high branches.
   Intoxication so
    certain it reminds you
     of your
deep mortality.

Flesh heart
 beating under all this
  imagism we take as
   real.

Afterwards, the
pen gets capped and

put away.

                                                12/15

NOISE IN THE KITCHEN

1

What if I went to check the
  noise by the cat-dish in the
    kitchen in the
middle of the night and it

wasn't the neighbor's Siamese cat marauding but a
timber wolf with fiery eyes and
   dripping fangs and a
huge black cloud of a
    body that
   filled the
     room with its
claws and
   teeth dug into me, my
whole life passing before me to the
tune of guttural snarls and
    deep musk of wild
      beast fur, or

what if it were a giant tapir in our
kitchen at night disinterestedly
crunching, solid and
  immovable as a
    rock until it
suddenly caught my
    scent and
   stampeded out into the

              night. Or if it were

a prehistoric horse, thicker and shorter, shaggier,
   Mongolian-looking, squat-legged, browsing,
      eyeing me through the
         centuries from the
      mouth of the
    cave of our
twentieth century house, whinnied a
      modern horse-whinny, stood up
once on its hind legs before
bolting out the
    door. Or back to

menace and the
tearing of teeth, a
  Kodiak bear, tall as the
house itself, head wedged
     underneath the
ceiling, engulfs the entire
      house in its
    brown-black bulk. Or what if it were

an evil djinn, long-featured, purplish-green,
  sly-eyed out the
     sly corners of its
        eyes, red-lipped, hoofed,
electric-charged, waspish, turns, looks, shrieks,
   sails forward and
      up through an
air not entirely of the

    house but at an
        angle up another
  dimension, blue-lit, a
            shaft of
disappearance enwrapping it
   completely
     away. Or what if the noise were a

whole nation of djinn with their cityscape stretching
   in dim Technicolor behind them, the main
     road up the
  hill, the strange-contoured
domes of meeting hall or
     mosque, the
       weird
angular trees like
   windblown
      match flames, everything erratically
still, hysterically
   motionless, silver-glowed, rustling,

by the
   cat-dish at
     night. Or what if it happened to be an

angel, not eating, but somehow having
made a noise, not a
   noise really, in fact it could be
the noise and the
   angel just happened to
      coincide, the angel was

passing, the
  house creaked, I
    went to
      see what it
was and a
  stairway of true
    Light embraced me and took me
up with it inside vast
  interstellar shafts of purest
    singing so that you never want to
      come to
  earth again, but keep

rising or
  going on
as long as
  measurement itself or even
    further, all of this taking place in

no place by the
  cat-dish at
night in our
kitchen on

Milpas Street in Santa Barbara one
middle of December, 1989, in the

Year of our Lord.

2

And what if we
   woke up in the
morning and there was no
     ocean only some
        rock, no

rain forest only some
   burnt wood, no more
slinky, secretive
    medicinal
      plants growing up
trees, only a
phenomenal gap, if we

woke up and there were no more
clouds only
   blazing light and
     suffocating heat, no more

birds only
glistening black-bodied
   insects with
     swift wings and
   venomous
      bites, what if we

went to the
   mountains but the
     streams had

     dried up, dry
stream-beds and
  river-beds, shale
 creeks and
    no
   waterfalls anywhere left on the
     earth at all, just silent
cliffs, no

animals, only
pictures of animals, all of them
legends and memories, descriptions in
writing, occasional
    motion pictures,

until we come to

waking up and there is only miles of unbearable
salt in all directions, miles of
cold crystal, and we
stand in the deafening glare of it unable to
move because we are

ghosts.

3

And as our
  coffins sail out under the
    moonlight what will we have

left on the
 earth to

remember us by?

12/15

NATURAL MONUMENTS

We all seem to want something
  darker, richer, higher, wider, to
swoop us outwardly or inwardly
  up, something decidedly
more coiled or serpentine, more
lavish in laziness, smoother, abler to spend our time
insouciantly, gazing at
natural monuments, becoming ourselves
natural monuments.

We talk as we sit in our smiles across the
table from ourselves pouring out our
life story in ten minutes, never quite
catching up with the present
predicament, adjusting the
occasion slightly or
  largely, we want to

stand up in sudden black hip boots and
stride off down an
  unknown avenue to an
    important destination, to suddenly
stand up with absolute determination and
    firm resolve and go off and
      do it *by God* and come back to
tell of it before it
crumbles, we want to
stand astraddle the entire creation with all its
unknown waterfalls and its

aboriginal lore, all the
   knowledge of the stars and their
     circuits across the
        heavens, the
depths of distant seas, we want to
   straddle those future
     geologic rearrangements, we want to

stand completely aside of everything in the entire
creation and let the Creator do all the
work as He intended, and we close and
open our eyes on schedule, opening them on a

vaster plane than we
   closed them to, closing them onto a

vaster more delightfully colored plane than we just
opened them on,

turn into fish or eagle in full flight, dive into deep
canyons on
   earth and in
     space. We were

created for multiplicity, to know the
varying Names of the Lord, we seek the
Magnetic North of His Unity to become

whole.

                                                  12/18

TYRANTS DRIVE PAST STATUES OF THEMSELVES

Tyrants are fleeing their countries in
   black limousines
driving past statues of themselves
huddled in back seats, counting
     on anonymity,

driving past statues of themselves
   erected during their salad days,
hoping against hope to get to the borders unrecognized,
their last days of iron-fisted action
backfired, explosions bouncing back
like repeated radio broadcasts
    in their hectic brains,

their loyal armies shooting into shouting crowds of comrades
backfiring until
giant shouting comrade-crowds filled palace doorways
      demanding
           tyrant blood

who now flee by back roads, at night, in
black limousines

driving past statues of themselves.

12/23

(Written while watching the execution of Romanian dictator Nicolae Ceaușescu and wife Elena on TV, machine-gun shot against a ragged wall.)

THE MYSTERIOUS DOOR

The mysterious door at the bottom of the forest may open
and you're in a supermarket, lost among
   watermelons, or

you enter a department store in search of underwear
and you're at the bottom of the sea, able to
  breathe easily, deftly
    maneuvering between
      giant clams, or

none of this may be true, life goes on
with the appearance of normalcy quite
regularly day after day, the

door opens at the
bottom of the stairs, you go
up and out and
catch the bus on
   schedule, return from
  work on schedule, go to
    bed on
   schedule, and there is

never a happy boa constrictor between your
sheets or
  molting in your
    bathtub, there are
never flamingos in pink flocks outside your kitchen
window in the

>   morning making a
>   page of pink
>   question marks in the
>   air with their
>   necks and
>   careful-footed stalking,

you never see the world slide away out of
focus outside the subway window only to slide
back into focus as the
    wastes of Mongolia with those
        bactrian camels shaggy as
    dust-mops grazing the
           sparse grass on
    gray-green tundra heights, blink and

then it's gone again, normalcy reigns, no
wonder fills your heart, renewed by the
wonder just around the
corner,

you turn the corner of the boulevard as you have for
twenty years every
    day on your
    way to the tobacconist, but today there are

Arab nomads camping in the
    square, shouting out the going
market prices for their
    camels, horses, sheep,
        mules, transistor

radios, CD players, 3 piece
   suits and
bedroom furniture on the
   mezzanine of the
     department store as you

go down the escalator and
out into
daylight again satisfied that

everything is
  snugly in
    place and there's a

smug smile on your
face that you know what

reality is after all, no one can

possibly fool you.

12/26

PRESUMPTION

As if,
   carved from light, you wouldn't
attract more light
     toward you, pulling it,
turn by turn, off its
       wire spool, sitting or

standing, by the
    beat of your
heartbeat. This is
      basic. This is

   landscapes
     speeding by.

Come to a
   sudden

stop.

                                    12/30

WHEN FRIENDS COME TO VISIT

When friends come you want to
   give them your
     best, drape ignited
glass rainbows over
     each of their
several ears, let them
   sparkle in their
     own light
glittered into life by the
   songs of your
     purest cascades.

You stand in a
   triangular door, half-
     moons huge as a
  house behind you,
there are
horses at full gallop the
   size of
     thimbles in the
       palm of your
hand but they
   pull you along
     anyway, over
matter's rude cobblestones. An

     eyeglass used by
       Louis Pasteur, hat worn by
William Blake, brim brightly

      curved against the
        wind, pair of
shoes Dante wore that show
    no signs of
      burning, coat dripping with
  lake-water that was
    Shelley's when he
      drowned, coat-pocket where his
final manuscript was found folded, whose
      last line reads:
        "Then what is life, I cried?"

Then the
shadow behind you of

saintly oracular presences with
bare feet whose noise along the
ground is heard
only by creatures of the
soil itself, deep in its

pure heart. That gift, held out on a

tray, scattered among the
    sweetmeats!

                                          12/31

WHEN WE LOOK UP AT THE STARS

When we look up at the stars
does a mental grate clank into place above us with
cartoon figures of stretched beasts, gods and goddesses
    floating sideways like aerobics in
        gelatin, or do hair-raising
  endless spaces fly out in every direction to no
       possible end of universe, spreading
          atoms apart in our
              own skins to see such
vast emptiness between twinkling lights? Green

sky, purple sky, sky of a black beast with
human face letting down its
   paw into our
     world and smiling with
        tropical sweetness, eyelids thick with
intoxicated slumber, lips as
   sensual as a
     night of love, anthropomorphized sky!

Or a doorway with little wooden
stairway slides open and
everything that ever was lets
    skyrockets of spiritual essences shoot high into
       immeasurable ethers, pebbles from
rocky mountain streams, tufts of grass from
rocky mountain ledges, islands which are
every person's personal garden float up like clouds
across the clearly visualized sky. Sky

in which we live more than on earth.
Sky like a vast glass warehouse where all the
forms that appear on earth sit waiting under
black sheets for the
command that will bring them rumbling out on
icy rails into full daylight, to become
  cataract, mountain-peak, pine, shore-bird,
    Jack-in-the-pulpit, shaman's potion, spoon.

Everything shimmering in
   invisible splendor in the
      sky! Even we there, like
  tubular lights, not
    defined but still
      definite, sudden
separations from undifferentiated brightness
into separate electric beings on legs with
jaunty smiles and hearts made for Paradise.

Roadways rarely frequented by foot-travelers
go right up into the sky. Faces

float there, answering the
more difficult questions. Propositions seemingly so
four-square and
      solid on earth get turned
    upside-down and poured out
tea-spouts as
  glistening water in the sky.

The sky rings with love's multiple echoes. Love's

multiple echoes are flung
   back and forth
      through the
         sky. The sky stretches

out on the backs of our hands at
sunrise, and if we
put our hands to our ears we can hear
love's reverberating
   echoes ring there in the sound of

light become flesh rubbing flesh as soft as
sand sifting down through sand in the
gigantic revolutions of the

gradually turning sky.

                                          12/31

TIME TO SING OF LOVE

Scatter aside the primitive shapes, *it's*
  time to sing of love!

The hand sweeps away
plume and robot, beauty and darkness,
terrible tall cliffs in natural ravines in arid territories
down which pack animals carefully tread, their
riders perched on rumps as mules' heads fall away in
    front of them at
      terrifying angles, only
  space spreading out below them
        like a threadless net.

I sit at my desk on two pillows in a
  cold room alone with children's
     voices going up the
    musical scales behind me, heart however
quiet, thinking of the

wineglass of bright love seen balanced on a pointed
mountain peak emitting its
  perfume, its color streaming
    out to transform the
      sky from
    tobacco black to pewter blue.
If we didn't drink from the wineglass directly, we
  smelled its thick odors —

and if we didn't smell its

    odors directly we smelled them on the
        breath of its drunkards
whose scent became sweet when it reached our
        nostrils. We didn't see the

night of shouting and grandeur in their
eyes. We didn't witness their rivers of blood
shed for love. Only the

thin scent of wine from that mountain peak, and
reports of its power. And then the

sticky light that spread from everyone's fingertips in the
    tavern, the stain of wine on
fingertips plucking fruit from God's branches and
putting their cool urns on our
tongues as pure
heat beat down.

A cloud just went past the sun.
The whole room's become dark.

Time to scatter aside the primitive shapes
and speak of love!

                                                1/21

IF WE ENTERED A WORLD

If we entered a world where a
  poem had never been written, a song
    sung, a prayer said, if I

imagined such a world for a moment from my
bed where I
  write this, sensations of
    sound pour into me (the street-washing
truck with its whirling brushes has
  just passed by)
and the clock ticks. We

lie back in a green cloud, along a
  green river, and
    bands of
      sunlight filter
        down.

A word never spoken in
  kindness, a
    hand given to
lift someone
  out of a
  mire, actual or
    mental. Can such a world even be

imagined? It's too late. A

poem's been written, a

song sung, a
prayer said.

The world has
never been the same.

1/4

ELEPHANT TUSKS

Tusks leaned up against a mud wall —
dangerous firelight draws curved stripes of
    bright orange along the right side of each —

the tight-lipped tusk-dealer is in a hurry —
he wants his money and he wants to be alone.
Each tusk tells too tender a story
about huge elephants on their sides with their
    tusks hacked off,
tons of elephant blood pouring into
      dust.

Each bill handed over to the
tight-lipped tusk-dealer becomes a
rifle in a firing squad that
    shoots him on the
        spot.

Loud chain-saws in the hands of greedy
    land-owners become the report of
firing-squads, and rainforests spring back into place,
    delicate canopies like hand-made lace but
much more delicate retaining their
    integrity, no
moss-thin thread
      broken.

Poisoned waterfalls become the
bloodstreams of the poisoners — they die ignominiously

on 40th floor offices —

wild waters clear, water-birds and zigzag jazzy rainbow
    fish rejoice.

Oil slicks on oceans spread on rhythmic ripples like
bad dreams,
enter the dreamers' consciousnesses and
   keep them from sleep. Are they the
owners of faulty tankers, or the
whole human race building huge empires dependant on oil?

The tusk-dealer knowingly kills for his profit.

Mankind's become a single person staring in
   disbelief at bad
newspaper headlines during breakfast.

How far out of balance we've become to push so much
of the planet's delicate structure to the
edge of destruction!

Millions of elephant tusks lined up against mud walls.

Millions of dollars turned into baked mud
    at the end of the world.

EVERYTHING'S ALIVE

for Tom Buckner

To walk on a slick blue plain like a polished tile
between broken Roman columns to face
a slate black sea, to stand stiffly on the
crystal shore with hair blowing back, stiff as a
horse's mane, stiff as
   many horse's manes. Then to seem as if
moving forward without effort of limbs, across the
horizon horizontally, like a

ship, profile in black against the
sheen of the black sea, a
soundless meditation, or the
shrill almost-silence of a
high hum. There is a

blue tinge to the scene, to the
sound, to the
moment, although all the
moments that led up to it were in
full color, the
   entire spectrum, and all the

moments leading away from this
moment might also be in
  full color, or perhaps only
    tinted black and white, a series, a
succession of sun-bleached polaroid snapshots taken from the
moment of this scene outward through the

rest of the life of this figure standing on the
margins of material existence with hardly a
care in the
world, hoping for
  benevolence from the
    elements and
  peace in our time, and true
intellectual light, and a
  heart that is a constant

escalator of rose-quartz warmed by the
passage of ascending and descending
celestial presences bringing
messages and carrying our
desperate petitions through all the

seasons of our life and in all
  geographical locations. Nowhere is not

sentient. Everything's alive. A spark as large as

the entire planet, or
  larger, animates every
ripple of the sea as well as every

vibration of our
vocal chords in
  parallel
    harmony.

1/7

SEATED AT THE PIANO

Seated at the piano, I write words. (I've

pulled the lid over the keys, it makes a perfect
desk of wood over ivory.)

Working at my job, the musings of my
heart are in tropics of possibilities beyond the
eight hours graceful duty dancing in
other peoples' spotlights. Tangly

tropics, with sudden
open spaces. Heavenly
greens and leaves as
large as lunchtime, as
savory-smelling as
myrrh on a round charcoal. Hidden

places no map shows except
between the wiggly lines.

We sit in our clothes
running
naked on a beach. We are
certainly
naked inside these
woven screens. But even our

consciousness forgets it, and we have
cloth arms and cloth-wrapped bends at our

supple waists, and we sit inside our

naked bodies, dwarfed or made
giant in the
moment's discursive
light-bulb filaments to tell a
tale that has no
beginning or
end, and our

consciousnesses forget shape and
substance and stretch
  non-arms out in non-air
to fly above earth's momentary
topographical arrangements.

These words are written down in
  deep pockets of
    silence, but like
underwater xylophones, pianos on the
  Titanic, their sound
    rises bubbling to the

surface of articulation between kindred souls
bending together to listen!

I should be writing popular songs.
Sharky lyrics to slink along 5th Avenue at
    midnight wearing
      hologram spangles to catch the
first light of gray dawn. But the

windowsill I dream I look out of looks out on
oriental marketplaces canopied in
light silver-blue mist. Humanity

bubbles up through the silence to the
surface and bursts into
voices naming all the meaningful
rendezvous possible to the
heart freed from its
cage in

Creation's first light to land on
white and black ivory
keys of this piano under the

wooden lid I now
  push open
    to play.

1/9

THE GARDEN IN THE PUPIL

The garden in the pupil of the i-
   singlass window with panthers dappled by
      sunlight under jagged banana leaves, pool-
drip, cool aromas, scrubby bits, elegant
hexagonal stones.

Hillocks with turtles, hillock and
  turtle become
    one in a certain
slant of light, shadows deeper than the
creases in your hand, ants crawling nonchalantly
up and out of them
  down your arm, bridges of natural
wood, ramps, stairways going right up to a
   tree trunk, stopping
dead at the
     bark.

The whole garden
revolves. Stones around
  plots become
     pearls. Fungus climbs
as petals fall. Through the

V of a branch in a white sky,
a hawk drunk on flight
flaps away.

1/10

I WAS GIVEN A BOX

I was given a box like a battered
    treasure chest,
it had sliding panels on all of its
      sides. I slide one

open. A face much like
mine blinks
  back at me. That's
   not the
one I want. I slide another

open. There are
meadows going far into the
distance between
purple-tinged peaks. A flash of
silver sits in the
distance which
  is the
    sea.
I could
take this one, and the
box would turn
  inside-out for me to

travel the meadow and
reach the sea.

This journey's not for me.

I slide another side
open and I'm
engulfed in
night, a thin red
outline sets itself
off from the
black and begins
to write Pythagorean
mysteries in
dream-like celestial
　script. The air is so
thin here I don't think I could
　live here for
long.

I open the last
side and I'm

back at the
beginning, only this time when I

slide the
sides aside each one is

different.

　　　　　　　　　　　　　　　　　　1/15

GOD'S FACE

God's face is hidden behind the
   black lamp on the

table in the
   corner that was

turned on in the
room when you

      died.

THREE DAYS, THREE WISHES

1

If I had only three days to live,
if I were given three wishes, and only
   three,
if I could choose another
    place to live anywhere
       in the world,
if I had it all to do over again, this one...

but none are true, and all. Entertaining the
idea of three days to live naturally makes us
existential. Would I just

get down on my knees for three days and weep
pools, or would I
want to see all my old friends to say
goodbye, or read the
Qur'an the whole time so that I might
float out on its *ayats* into
light, or would I want to

spend my last days and nights in hospitals
slicing the full moon into edible wedges
   for sick children,
gather my family around me, Job-like, to
impart last messages, receive last
messages clear, or would I want to
go somewhere, like Mecca, sit there, pray there?

The world and all its allures would effectively be
over for me, desires to see
mountains or oceans, or hear
music from a gamelan in Bali, or an
orchestra in Fez, or sit for a single

moment in a rainforest to maybe see the
perfect jewel of the night-blooming Cereus that comes out just
once a year in the
middle of the
Amazon and then is
    gone, to sit in the
  damp, hot, alive, in the
    midst of
life, matter,
    enthrallingly
  fused of beauty and depth, dark
    endlessness of
      profusion — its

allure would be
  gone. The tree frogs will
    blink beyond
me. The
  deforestation
    continue until man
sees his mistake, maybe
    too late. I would be

jerking my thumb under my green neon
suspenders, heading out the

door of the
air, looking

back with a
meaningful
glance, not

winking exactly, but neither

looking as if the look would
last forever. I would go

mix myself with the
dust motes floating in that

beam of sunlight down that
dark trail next to the

silent bulldozer.

2

Granted three wishes, like
   transparent vases on tall stems filling with
hallucinatory smoke, focusing clearly on
true pictures which come to life in altered states
such as illness being cured, wishing for a
vehicle of continuous efficacy so that
these three wishes could be prolonged —

a wand to make things happen for the good
even if their immediate outcome is
terrible — but this usurps God's
perfect timing of events, lifts
corners of covers fallen down across future scenes
where uncertainty is the
condition for certainty, knowing the
   Source of surprises, holding onto the

Turner of the kaleidoscope not the

falling broken pieces of
   colored glass inside the
illusorily mirroring mechanism.

3

I want to pour myself out onto this page
like water down a drain
and come out on early morning fields getting my
   socks soaked with dew. Anywhere else to

live on earth but where I am now. Yet the
shadow would be the same, against different
walls. The hand reached out from my
covers in the morning, with the same pulse
running down my arm. Blank siphons of

possibility, fabrications of mind only! Smoke-stacks
out of anywhere, the ache in the

same place in the heart. Two stags with criss-
    crossed antlers face off for
        prestige. The dew on my
socks is on their
   antler-tips, their
     snorts make steam, fine white
       water-spray against
         gray morning haze.

"The mummy we are, wrapped in tight-wound bands
and laid in a box, is, down some
musty stairs, past the
  pillars of the curse, as vast in its way,"
said the old immigrant sitting on the
    tumbled lintel stone, *"as the entire*

starry ocean above us, or the
  wet sky sloshing at our shores." Faith in the

light at the pointed archway to our peculiar pyramid
is what keeps that dimension alive, illuminates
its indecipherable walls.

To knock on any door
with a thirst for strangers
is enough to be let in
by the keeper of unknown facial expressions who

hands you the key. Eyes light up like
ancestral fires with the absolute
soulfulness of humanity when you meet

face to face with the
assuager of sorrows. No

corridor is too long to go down then. No
distance more than a happy
  succession of thoughts.
But with the right footwork, right foot always
in the lead, heart held high in the
hand like a lamp, intellect humming like a
  smooth engine, corridor becomes
courage-door, door opens, you feel

fresh air against your whole face for once after
four centuries. Cord of war. Accord of air.

Can we pour ourselves out to be
elsewhere than where we are?

Moving from side to side. Hawk-glance

gliding over hills. First one side, tilt, then
the other. Eyes on each
side of our
heads. Hills in rolling humps to the
sea. Sloshing raw

starlight on the neatly
  trimmed edges of our
    shores.

4

If I had it to do all over again

I would write this

poem all over again.

> 1/24 -1/29

THE NIGHT FLOATS

The night floats between the
   twin tips of its sleepers
above bright blue lakes, against a pure
    silver backdrop with
       tiny holes poked into it to let
         the light from
   greater distances through onto the
faces of the floaters like
  long black weeds with
     naked human bodies stretching across the
        entire known universe.

No one is actually asleep. Even the dead
are looking.

The sleepers rummage through mythological warehouses
trying on horse's heads, bat-wings, gladiator visors,
abandoned gossamer, try out languages both
    obsolete and arcane, from the
whispering syllables of
   tiny groups of Amazonians to the
gruff shouts of nomads in Mongolia, a word from
  here added to a
    word from there, it's a
video arcade of vocabularies like the
Tower of Babel outfitted with
  yackety
        flickering TV screens all
  facing each other, and ribboning arms are

outstretched to hold hands underwater, a
continuous bridge of sleeper's arms across the globe undersea
with pulses telegraphing humanity's heartbeats to
each other across space, the
   rhythmic essence of matter, heart-code
deeper than language-nodes, telegraph of
     human vulnerability in the face of

the black door at the horizontal bottom of sleep, under the
fraying edge of night worn out with so much
weeping and rolling, snoring and
 lovemaking, loneliness and ecstasy of
   spiritual explosions into realms of
      utter harmony,

in a night like cracked leather, a night like a

cracked leather suitcase inherited from a
rich uncle from an
  earlier century carried through
train-car after train-car until it
sits down and looks out Minnesota
   windows at
  farm-houses passing in the
      night under a
    cold full moon

where the cows also sleep, pigs and
horses and butterflies, and the

night floats between tips of

living sweetness and hunger like a
   sticky web covered with
      tiny
   dew-pearls of
      earliest morning.

2/2

EYES PLANTS

Chase the brazen stag
  over a hill —
what a lovely
    halcyon image, green as
      green velvet, hoof-sounds
        clattering on
          shale,
darting eyes, ours and the
    stag's, for
fear, for the
    chase, into the
embroidery. It

hangs on a barren wall.

What started as a tip of
antler soon became a scene.
A town in the distance, spreading
    out around a lake.
Gray light. Late light. Dark
deeps in the
    lake. A
      winter
        scene. A boulder

man of tumbled stones comes
out and sits on a stone.
His face is rock. His thoughts are

long, slow thoughts. He is as
naked as the
earth. His feet go

miles underground. Petroleum
pumps through his veins.
His memories are short
over long spans. An idea
pops into and
  out of his
    head and it's
a hundred-thousand
  years. He is

unfazed by time, and the
dying into
  stillness of the
dead, or the

leaping of
  stags.

He is
  unfazed by
    time, shadows of
outrage on a
    white wall, sizzling
smoke of accommodation,

peace like a
  loose white

   cloth settling slowly
      down over
         stone. His

face is not a
   human face, he sees

more than
   we do. Stone
expressive of
   stone. Eyes

plants.

                                                          2/5

MUSIC

1

Ahgh! If only I could
   just write music! I feel like a

raw bumpkin who's been to the
other side of the mountain above his
village when I write, seen
   valleys where the capitol shines
      with its multiple golden cupolas, spires like
heavenly knitting needles, light glaring off the
sides of official buildings, from the
blaring white squares of a hundred glass windows,

and I've come

running back, stumbling down gravel-slides, skinning my
ankles on brambles, in haste to stand

babbling half-incomprehensibly on the outside of the
plate glass between that vision and the villagers,

gesticulating, using bursts of words, exaggerating,
trying out new ways to help them
see what I'm driving at, but I have to

admit it, nod kindly, look briefly ignited,
smile at each other and back at me consulting,

my efforts as seemingly fantasy as the pictures in this very
poem itself, so that when the

night comes they shuffle away, and the
dark descends back of the
mountains as well, blanketing even what
   lies on the other side and was so
gloriously seen, in the same banal darkness.

I would have a steady tremolo of strings, like
night-creatures, like insect-buzz, like the soft snapping of twigs, or
the walking through woods of all
humanity in bare feet over dry pine-needles,

then out of that texture a note would rise, the
color of gold, a glass note, transparent and slick,
not container but transmitter of
sound, and everything would

break away into aerial components, atoms almost
visible in the air like active
sparks around a campfire, only they're the

atoms of everything doing their dance of joy, in
   meticulous textures, inter-
      weaving and tugging at each
other's rhythms enough to make
      a fabric of universe where no

seam shows, no
   beginning or end, our

own selves singing in the
    weave.

2

Then, for sorrow, the low twang of cello-strings, the
low-down whale's weight of
human notes so low no voice, not even those
Tibetan monks with three bull-frog octaves to their bassos,
can reach to engulf all humankind's dear
sorrow in one brown river washing through
earth and sky, past curve-tipped roofs of
Canton, through wide-eyed nights of
Nigeria, lonely forested acres of
pine-tree Canada, Fiji Isles old man lost
wives and children, last one with the
lore, sitting in faded levis on an atoll,
    white-haired, heart weeping
large as the sea he looks out on, dry-eyed,
singing the old songs completely
through to himself one last time
  to the equally white-haired
      sea.

Which is the background
noise to the other, sorrow or joy? Which is the

fabric of truth our existence passes in front of?

Which is the

widest sea the other's
    absorbed in? And if it's

sorrow, does joy have no
    defensible existence? And if it's

joy, can we
    fix our gaze past the
        black gateposts and
miles of identical Hiroshimas smoking white ash
        at our horizons?
Or is it purest existence itself that is the
long-held note, constant to our

    major and
        minor melodies,
    crying and
        rising chords?

Bright white
    flakes hit moving
tips of black water. Black defining
    brush strokes
        slap along sliding
            white crests.

OUR HOUSE IS FLEXIBLE ENOUGH

Our house is flexible enough for the
   great wind to blow through it,
rattling windows, banging interior
      doors, even making
   cupboard doors scuffle a little in their
         frames, and I'm
glad for it. I hear the

great wind around us like a
huge up-curving arch of surf that completely
covers over us, spindly
powerful arms of wind, like
indefatigable ivy tendrils
come in through vulnerable cracks, snake their
vibrant web looking for
   things to rattle in the
      space they increase in, the

wind entering the house in quick currents, then getting
fatter and
   wanting to get out!
Where does such a
   rhinoceros wind come from, and
      where is it going?

Savage vagrant, it
   knocked over a
      framed photo of
Afganistan I had propped up against the

    unused fireplace by
slithering right down the
    chimney!

The homeless can't curl
up in it for warmth out
   there, where
palm-trees shake their
  heads like voodoo
dancers when the
   trance is on.
    Dead arms come
hurtling to the
   ground. Dead
twigs and branches
   thrown around.
Now it's increasing — sounds like sea-waves come
right up the shore to our
   house
    ten blocks from the
     sea to shake the
wiry scraping leaves of
outside trees.
And it
  could come full blast out of
heaven. Could

  slam through the
   spaces left open in
matter's resistant surfaces, brittle
    thoughts and their

    shadows. Could

bring its vaporous giant corkscrew down to our
dimension from maelstroms up in clouds so huge
whole continents could be
   carried along in its wildly
      spiralling arms. A

wind's whale breath keeps our
planet in place, so
powerful it keeps all the
planets in place, the
   sun and other
   stars. A wind so

vast it's become
   serene, and all these
     tiny cyclones, including our
own day and night breathing for an
      entire lifetime, are like

one sparkle on a
   wave held up
    in the
air before
     falling.

IN A WORLD WITH NO TIME FOR POETRY

In a world with no time for poetry
   we still have to die.

It would be so convenient if we could just
turn in our badge with our
     full-color picture on it, go into a room
   set aside for that purpose at the
     corporate office
and evaporate, our desk left in order,
  instructions on the
    computer for the
      one who fills our
        shoes.

But the earth itself is alive, its roots and its tendrils,
and even minerals are part of the food-chain
    in the deep dark loam.
Air pushes itself in, shoving aside 40 story buildings
like a vaporized Jolly Green giant
   to swirl around the
     newly enamored, the
incessantly dejected, the old man watching at his window
      for death,
the young girl wearing it next to her
   skin on the
  inside of her
     coat.

Our bodies are ticking, their time is limited where they can

carry out the wishes and desires of the
unlimited spirit, but while they're here

they get welts on their legs, exude fluids and
  perfumes, live in a
    strictly practical world, no time for
nonsense, while their

hair grows in ghost-land as long as the
anchor rope of the phantom galleon,

minute mites like birds in branches settle down on our
  eyelashes, thoughts like
ribbons of incandescence curve through us as
  wide as the Niger,

and as we sit the walls around us become
  obsolete, the hillside that
    emerges as the
  house dissolves, full of
unused warrens and
    ant-entrances, blows away from

underneath us in a fine powder heading back to
    The Fashioner.

FIFTEEN MINUTES TO WRITE THIS

I wake up at 3:30 in the night with my
   beard soaked in sleep's slobber
having to pee, and
in the dark conceive of
   writing this poem, so I return to my
bed to do so. I fell
asleep writing the last one, actually

dozed right off in the
  middle of a line, and thought now about
piercing upward through the
  oasis membrane of
    waking in the
middle of the night, not wanting to
wake up entirely, I should
   write within dream's kingdom to keep myself
     partially asleep.

Saints sail on luminous half-moons in half-light past me,
the ones who
   purposely get up in the night to
   pray, wet themselves with
cold water on
  arms and face, but I'm
sitting up to write this, eyes still
   stuck with sleep, piercing
up through
  sleep's astrodome, the
others in the

    house still tightly
wrapped in night's
    cocoons, glowing
lozenges on
  long leaves bouncing imperceptibly
higher or
  lower in sleep's
    woods, most of the
town asleep, perfect
  time for
    invasion, wake up to find city streets
occupied by Martians or
hungry Nicaraguans (wearing
  threadbare clothes, holding
    wooden rifles).

But I long to
  poke northward in this
waking sleep, like an
ocean liner with porthole lights be-
    dazzling the
  night sky with yellow-
    white rows of circles of light —

snag the consciousness of sleepers as far
away as Timbouctou and Shanghai in my
    sleep's net, go
lugubriously seaward with the deep-throbbing
    engine growling most un-
      humanly the Creator's Name that
        stirs the

                guts and gets us all
                    reoriented
    true north in our
    blood's compasses,
            heading out to a
        sea actually sky, living in the blue-domed
                earth as in a
                    ship's cabin,
    navigating by
        stars as familiar as
    freeway headlights
            streaming toward us — heading out and out toward
    territories totally
            unheard of, where we will all be there
    already, but a
        bit more
            enlightened, not

    asleep at all, and obviously
            better for it, living on
                habitable and
        human-sized
            islands of
    materialized deep consciousness, leaves that
        talk and stones that
            hum quietly to themselves, birds that glide
    amused
    slowly overhead. Fish making slow-motion arcs above the
            surface, then in the depths. This isn't

    pie in the sky, it's more like

emerald
   sherbert that
      melts in the
   sun, more like
lagoons of half-sleep, where I'd
rather wake up than here
   in my bed, the city's actual
mechanical sounds going on and
      off all around me, water
charging through pipes under the
      house, something roaring
muffled in the
   distance outside —

   bunched congregations of

   clouds like a cappella choirs, bands of
jiggling light like something to
      wear, the
   night like a
      noble companion you can
   safely confide darkest
secrets and weakest
      fears to, but it only sits perfectly

composed with an
ancient exquisite face, smiling your
   own smile back at you.

It took me exactly fifteen
minutes to

   write this.

I face the clock around, and turn off the
   lamp to go

back to sleep.

1/16

UP A RAMP INTO THE FUSELAGE

Up a ramp into the fuselage,
   stairway up to lift-off onto celestial
      tropical territory, leaves arching leaves
so red and orange they make sky colors pale,
   bird plumage bleached, Bird of Paradise flower-petals like
      gray fog, we're entering

the machine shop of eternal archetypes, gelatinous
   shadows like slicks of
     oil and water-twists forming
doorways in tar-huts, windows in Austrian palaces on pointed
     mountain-peaks, cut hedge
       corridors in garden labyrinths,
everything anyone can think of —

the experience of the blind, deaf, and dumb
genius saint whose heart is brighter than a
billion cut diamonds — that
   sense of life is one of the archetypes
created by the Merciful to live among
as much and as
   real as big-leafed lianas twisting up
     dark Amazonian trees —

the moustache of the evil lieutenant he
twists and retwists with a vengeance —
that's in there as well waiting to be
   worn by someone fitting this
      superciliousdescription,

as well as the soft, feathery, powdery cool fingertips of the
sleepless girl who lives near the Chicago subway station
    whose touch actually
heals broken wing'd cage-birds, grandmothers with
      rasping coughs, desperate lovers, healed by just one
  electrifying touch from those
    tapered fingers —

that's an
archetype of the Creator also in His
    factory inside Invisible Mountain!

Two people clink glasses on a balcony in Switzerland
and communicate something between their
   eyes that can't be
     translated into
any medium. A baby looks
  cross-eyed and then
    straight-eyed at you and for the
first time in its
    new-born heart sees something that will be
      counted on as
     a build-up of its
  peculiar
    reality forever. And that same

baby years later, on a
top floor behind a
  closed door, in
    meticulous
spiritual instruction, goes past that

interpretation for the
first time, un-
   tangles, dis-
     lodges, de-
  mystifies reality to its

burning actual glow of true direct
manifestation of the
   Creator's raw
     impulse of live
eternity in time

and that taste of it is so
extraordinarily strong it brings on shooting shafts of
   ecstasy, shoots the
     Seer into

tropic celestas, where broad-leafed lotus discs of
     harmonious vapor suspend the
experiencer's weightlessness forever
on a pool of
   trickling non-water which anyone at any

moment on earth can
dip his or her
   cup into and

drink.

2/17

THE IMAGINED LANDSCAPE

1

The imagined landscape flips to the inside of the eyelid
that closes down over the world,
sea-surf as eyelashes, the entire
   galaxy a giant pupil gazing on itself.

An eye that is the galaxy
looks across the table at the wall that is
    endless space, out a
      window that is
   a companion universe, dollies down a
 corridor that has
   rooms at each side, the door
opens on one and a Mandarin figure in stiff
   emerald robe is gloating over a
     map of uncharted seas.

Open another and ancient men and women sit by the
side of an open pit and gaze down at the
hairy mammoth fallen into their trap,

open another and
  vague amoebic forms
float in the air into each
    other's circumference and
   out again, humming
      weirdly,

even the absolutely
  transparent atmosphere we
    live in is an

imagined sea of light inside a thought that
ignites us into action.

2

We are all at the
  end of the world
  sitting on wooden benches overlooking the
    perfect breathing
      water of the sea
under sky like the smooth inside of abalone, pearly
    clouds swiped in leafy strokes
      in pink and gray, and the
sea sighs and re-sighs its breathy stillness, and we sit and

cross and recross our legs to get even a
little bit comfortable in this
  life before we're
    out of it.

Will these same eyes look out on the sea forever?
Will this consciousness with its
  clarities and
    lapses remain after its
shell has dissolved into the
  sloshy froth-sound going on so

     constantly in this world, or the
lights in long ripples down there across the
   stoic water?

Are the
  eyes the eyes of the soul,
so when the
   soul flies out will it
     fly out
   looking out these
     same eyes? Or is there
then
no looking? Sea going
back and
  forth without
   us? Oh

clouds curving up and brush-stroking along the
   sky, and
rock covered in succulents,
   reeds and
     grasses in clumps, whipped
by sea-winds, thoughtless of these
     ponderous questions, eyeless from the
start, but a part of
   creation's
    seeing of
   itself under
    white
     sky!

3

Around an
   unforeseen corner you may find
the Place of the Black Veils

which is not a place, but the
   advent in the normal
     chronology of your day of the
totally unexpected — with
       flute music.

Lorelei, or the
   Ghosts from the Five Islands will not
shoot you with their lugers.
Neptune may invite you in to
   dine, his
     tall fork ready for T-Bone, bubbles
cascading from your
  mouths up to a
    glassy surface above which you can see the
      yellow sun shine.

What world are we
   in at
  any given moment? Down below the
up above is upside-down to your
     upturned normal realm. But no one can be

sure for long when even
stately trees trade places in the formal Garden while the

      minuet rings. And logic,

worn down by cares and over-popularity, whose
flowing coat has turned to wood, runs tapered
fingers through thinning hair at the
   end of a century whose
torpor and terrors are at least a
     match for earlier centuries, if indeed they do not
        exceed them.

Yet at
  any moment the
    whole thing could pry loose, and there you'd
be free-floating
     beside the hundred or more
tons of your
seemingly still ship going a couple of
  hundred miles an hour in one-
     dimensional
       blackness. Certainly no
sound to speak of, no
  dove's music, no
    crashing of
     waves. The

drumming of your
  blood against the
tunnels of their
    veins. And you float

like drumming blood within the wall-less

    tunnel of space with light at
        both ends going

full blast, and you may retrograde
    backwards or
        fantasize forwards to
           identical

light in different
    places, but otherwise

the same.

Meanwhile
you may turn an unforeseen corner and be
   faced with incomprehensible
     music, Mozart at the
keyboard of an
   absurdly small
      spinet doing amazing
   spider routines with his
    fingers up and down the
      polished keys with a
melody so poignant it breaks all our

hearts in unison! No

plaster mask will be made of your
   astonishment. You could as easily be

climbing Mount St. Helens before the

    eruption as sitting down to
      tea with the Lord Exchequer on
        Fleet Street, but you

don't, frog-suit or not, make moves that are
too abrupt or unusual. And the world stays
pretty much the
   same. The bird's feed needs
blowing out each
   morning over the
front step, the
   dust collects in
strange places on the
   rug, rolled in
rug-rope tufts of
    lint. But in our

hearts out the
   hut-door the usual
     scene could
change at any
   moment and we'd be

composing massive Operas on "The Truth"
on a beach in Tahiti, or second story suites above
the Grand Canal, water reflections

fluttering white gleams in ripples of light
   like Morse Code messages on the
     villa's flaking ceiling

while a cat uncurls its optimum length and
   stretches, becoming briefly

divinized in a stray light shaft before

curling back to
    sleep.

                                                        2/22-23

YOU ARE WHAT YOU EAT

I'd like to write a poem as
   perfect as an antelope, with all its
grace and energy, its
    big black eyes round as an
      insect's, but
beautifully soft, intense, alert, its essential body
    able to fly fast over
   dunes, able to shift
     directions in a
       flash, compact, able to

bound with all the coiled
   strength of its
    legs, outrun the
tiger, ears back, horns carried
   high, graceful in
  panic as in
     repose, nearly flying over the
      slopes, the
   tiger closing in
behind it, the antelope watching completely
   forward until the
     end, the tiger finally making one last lunge and
pouncing on it and in
   an apocalypse of dust the poem

     meets its
   destiny in the teeth of the tiger's
     superior power, the tiger's

easy lordliness, that face of
    ecstatic stripes, that
Chinese Opera mask within which,

sated, the antelope's
own black eyes gaze calmly now

out across
vast expanse.

                                                              2/24

CHILD IN PAIN

To see your child in pain is
   such a
      haunting thing, they are so
barely articulate, so
   imperfectly self-aware, they
call out for help, for you to
   heal them magically and their call may be their
      first glimpse of your
helplessness, how we ourselves are
reaching our own thin arms out of the
   abyss, bodies pressed together as in a
      dark elevator going
down into the mine, and here they are
   hoping we'll know
      exactly what to
         do. Our

son came in, his face all red, his
   eyes squeezing out
      tears of
         pain like a
master chef squeezes out
   last lemon drops onto
      something cooked, in this case
his poor thin twelve-year old body raw with
   inner gas, holding his
side dramatically, unable to
   walk, stumbles with
   help into our

bed, barely
   able to
lie down, hollow

space of child's
  consciousness coming to
    grips with the down-sliding
suck of
  cosmos, how
sweet God has made us for the
  most part
   to feel no
    pain, our
nerve-endings mostly
   shielded, or
  buffered, or

whatever it is that makes this
  exquisite mortal body so
   able to go
    on day after
day for the
  most part O.K. until

drastic agony strikes, iron-
   hammer blows to
hot organs and
  hard bone. We feel the
  sharper edges of the
material universe inside
   us, like the

sharp bridle and bit in a newly-broken horse's mouth
   that is used to
forcibly turn him

into the
   wind.

2/27

TIME-DROUGHT

1

We're in a water-drought, but could there ever be
   a time-drought?

Time used
   sparingly, if at
      all? And only for
   really important
         occasions.
Could time be recycled so that
   past time would come
      round again for re-use, erased, but
         the same? Could time be
recycled, purified of its salts and softeners?

Or "gray time," from
   time that's been
used up for habitual domestic pursuits? Could we
   collect it in buckets?

Time saved and stored from
   time wasted? Time
   dripping from those ancient long
      summer afternoons, come down
transparent tubes in a faint green fluid?

Could all time we've spent in our lives
   waiting in line, in airports and

doctor's offices, be rechanneled through whatever
    misty terrestrial or
extraterrestrial tunnels time gets filtered through to

reappear in its measureless, unstoppable band all
  around us in air and within our
    delicate capillaries, the same time

clicking like soft crickets as it passes into the
timeless river behind or in
    front of us, blocks and cycles and

tight coils of it reappearing reusable and non-
      degradable as we

move in it,
  loving it or

hating it?

2

A time-drought, when
  time runs dry,
a distant
  sound between
    trees in a
  wood of time sinking
    down into the
      ground. Cocoons

held up because of a
   scarcity of time, suspended in mid-
     process somewhere between
          grub and
          butterfly, the

cup of liquid sand held up to the
  lips at
     desert's edge, suspended
until the
   time-drought ends and the

hour-glass flows again through its
    needle's eye
       opening from
   one empty side to the
      other,
in
 empty and
    full successions
       forever, and time

floats visibly up to our
   eyes from
      within, slow, smooth

time in dots on a jetty in the sun with
   wine-flask of light eating
      french-bread by the
         glittering river of

time that flows out past our
   ten-toed
      feet to the

         sea.

2/27 -28

THE CUP THAT RECORDS THE EVENT

In the distance you can see
  little pink domed houses
    on the surface of each leaf,
the tracks of sea horses dragging a
feather carriage through the sand,
an eruption as
    beautiful as a sunset.
If you squint across the sea against the hot sea-glare
you can just make out the tame
   succession of continents in a
     half-moon row, like ducklings following their
mother duck, like
  flashing computer impulses, and just above, as if
    reflected upside-down from below,

a silver silhouette in the sky of a
cityscape complete with rushing
  crowds across streets before the

night catches them
  out without their recognizable
    features on.
Everything is fleeting. Milk seeps in under our
   doors. Chairs stand on their
own four legs.
Conversations stop at their
   natural punctuation.
Everything seems to stay
    suspended in the air forever.

Every conceivable beast has come down to the
   dry waterhole to drink, and look
      disappointed, and

die.
Gnats hover like a lost city
an inch above the grass.
The wind saunters. The mind
    wanders.
We contain multitudes.

Fish spill out of our mouths
   happy to arrive in open
      waters at last between

the yes's and no's of human discourse.
If everything lasted or didn't last so long, or at least
as long as a camel driver's song, or as long as
smoke between buildings reflected in
    forty stories of glass, of
      light flashing off the
circle of a
glass-rim, off the lipsticked lips that
   touch that glass-rim, opening
to sip and
   closing to
      swallow,
off the mysterious moist
   organs in the
      dark of the
body, lying next to each other in an

    orderly jumble, not quite like in those
multi-layered cellophane diagrams in French dictionaries, but
        just nearly —

if everything lasted longer than the
   eyeblink that
     catches them in
mid-flight, then this
   creation wouldn't spin on one leg beneath a

single gaze of pure silver,
wouldn't spin on a
   table-top suspended above an

infinity of edges, wouldn't be
   satisfied with
contemplating it-
    self in its
own rotation, wouldn't fill

page after page of rough
   manuscript with song, or

channel after channel of
4 dimensional space with its
3 dimensional pictures as the

sea parts and we hustle across, holding tight to
   the handles of our
    final valises, Pharaoh's army's

horse hoofs beginning to hit the
    hem of the
distant surf as he

enters in hot pursuit, our
whole case lost at last,

but won in the bas relief of happy transfigured souls
at the base of the cup that
    records the event, held
up before being drained to the dregs

in a

mist of fading light.

2/28

WHEN YOU BECOME NAKED

For Malika on our 10th Anniversary

When you become naked a strange thing
   happens to the world.
The powdery
   cleavage of your breasts makes yellow light
      lie lightly along a
         canyon's ridge.
The way your legs articulate to your back
makes wind move
   differently through trees, leaves tumble
      strangely through the
         branches and
           land among the rocks.
Your back's curve makes the curves of
musical instruments come
   alive with a
      silkier sound, cellos leaning against
         red velvet vibrate a sweet
      sensational tone, your

belly, where we
   listen with our
      ears against its
         coolness, a fox family
huddles in its warren, the young
   foxes making their pointed red
      ears go straight as they
   sniff and

        listen for
     friendly sounds.

Your breasts make a whole orchard become
   fruitful overnight, to the
      great joy of the
         poor Anatolian farmers in the
heights whose
   orchard it is. Your

legs lie like low mountain ranges on top of each other,
behind the knees are cups that fill with
rainwater in the rocks,

your womb a secret place of mercy under moss,
entrance and exit both to
   creator and
      creature in
         this world, your

whole body bowled around it like a
sacrificial altar sculpture, incurring a little

blood and a little libation.

But the body has a face, your face, your
only face, seen in a
   train-window as it
      looks out on the
         scene, seen
      surrounded by white

    pillows on the bed, your
        hair fluffed out
           around it, asleep,
              eyelids

closed, mouth in
repose. The earth grows

silent when your
mouth is in

repose. And
darker when your

two eyes close.

                                                      2/29

LANGUAGE IS A DOOR

Language is a door, you
  swoop out of or
    stutter down stairs into
      dirty snow.

Language is an eye-wink across a crowded diner.
  You get up or you
    remain seated. It chips large
tiles off the mosaic of empty space.

Utterance hits the mark when the
  canary's song changes in its
    cage deep in the
mine from inhaling carbon gases to
    singing ecstatic song.

Windows sail through the door with sheepfold scenes on
    green hillsides etched inside them. A

face from nowhere with wild African eyes, almond-slanted,
    silver-blue, gazes in at us in our

meandering entertainments. What have we

done? Closets of cadavers standing straight up in
linen suits wait to be
    opened or
      locked up forever. The corporate

lexicon has only one page and it's
   full of abbreviations. Where's the

sacred wood in all this
   texture, the
      tangle of greenery out from which bounds
   the moss-covered many-armed
hooded wanderer whose
   mouth is a flame,
whose wings are ladders made of copper, lined on all their
   rungs with
newly-drowned sailors. They have
   sighted the mermaids and mermen and they
      will not be denied.

Language is a shipwreck late at night on a night with
   no moon, one
   crack then
silence, both ships go
   down in
total silence, all
      hands lost.

Lost entirely. Even their own

mothers don't remember their
   names.

Language is that silence.

Language is a single Babylonian harper

   black as night in
      gold arm-bands and
leaf loin-cloth, sitting on a
      single pylon,
playing over and over the same
ten-note melody to the end of the
      fifty-first century.

Afterwards
the hearers can't remember what they've
    heard. The harper's heart is

filled with sound and meaning caught from the

giant glass dipper of light that pours
   all language out.

That pours all language
   deep into our heart.

3/6-7

SCARF OF SWEET VISIONS

1

Scarf of sweet visions thrown across the landscape,
 I call on you!
I want my hearers to settle in their chairs
 knowing they'll be treated kindly.
I keep seeing a
 landscape with maybe a tiny figure
  in the distance, walking along,
 crossing fields by fences.
Largely green. Green hills, bushy trees, blue sky,
 mid-summer warm, high buzz of
  insects occasionally in the
   air, idly, their
   little musical figures, right near
    our ears,

this whole vision eaten by a whale, a
 sea-monster of monstrous size and
  demon disposition, one
swipe at the continent and its
 huge mouth closes
  over from above and
up from underneath taking farm-houses, cities,
 whole governments in hyperbolic meetings in large
  rooms with mahogany
   tables, but it's not a

real whale, it's made of yellow

    fire, it curves up around
        cornfields and lakes, engulfs the

wanderers and
  sojourners while its
    objective almost
      benevolent eyes gaze outward
          unafraid,
and our sweet reverie is
    shattered by this

black slice of death down through the
delicious elegance of green fields and blue skies,

and we are the distant
    figure walking there, come

forward in a flash to look
    face on into the

horror!

2

But it all happened so
    suddenly that what have we
      got to do but
        walk on, and we

do, and the trees and things alongside the

    sides of our
        peripheral vision also travel, until we are

walking with wave-crest and squawk, bird-
dart and squirrel-curl of
    tail as it
scrambles up a
  tree. The
    whole world moves
      along with us as we
  walk, tops of

cityscapes disappear below the
  horizon as if
    sinking, lower edges of
      clouds reflect back
pictures of gardens in
  circular
    formation whose
gateways are our own
  heart-beats, our
    foreheads are dark
  hedges arched above the
      gate, our
bodies are the faintly groaning sound of
    growth from
      root to bud and down to
  ground again, without
    cease.

Circular garden

revolving through our
   beings without
      cease!

3

O whole universe moving as we
   move, you are a
      gnat caught for a fragile
         moment in the
light, how can you be
      blamed? Wing-beat and
         feeler-wiggle, and what goes on inside your
inscrutable head, surrounded by
   shell. Universe of
      wavering fronds, ferns, friendly or

unfriendly thongs, thorns, twine, winding tendrils
   around edges, through
      surfaces, tingling and
wiggling
   underground, looking only for the farthest
reach of their
      destiny, to be root to the tips of their
   roots, bud and flower to
         petal-tip and aroma-nose, to brain of the
one bending down inside its tender
         vulva to inhale that
smoking smell, until whole
   rose-gardens burst into

      bloom in the
brain as fresh if not
    fresher than the
        one outside, in which identical

strangers also bend to
   inhale
     universes waiting to be
       transmitted through electrical
   impulses like long-distance
      telephone messages that sound like they're coming from

just down the block! *Interior Rose!*

Intimate petaled apparel of
  universe we live and
    die in, flesh
ignited and quenched by
     desire, light
    bathing our final

limbs and the little shock of momentary
   death freezing for a
     solid second our

infinite flutter of eyelids.

                                              3/8-9

PEOPLE AT A POETRY READING

There are people in the front row dying of strangers,
people at the sides with labyrinths upturning giant
   iron platforms in their heads, cascades
      rushing down their sides as they
         tilt, the whole earth-shelf
   capsizing under the
         strain. Others
live in tightly furnished rooms so as not to
float too freely out of their
   one-time bodies, and they bring this
     crowded aisle everywhere they
go as if a
large mummified elephant were placed by
obedient attendants wherever they
pause or sit, to stand above them with its
stuffed trunk laid lightly across their necks.

Others are fine in shaded woods or parks, they
  sit here in straight-backed wooden
     chairs but there's
       dappled sunlight in their
  hair, they smell like
    earth's own perspiration.
Deep musk of crevices and armpits, hair like
  sparrows' nests, wood-shavings.
Earth clinging to their beings in spirit
the way their bodies cling to their
   souls in
physicality. Others

stand in moonlight, lay on marble benches by
Grecian white pillars in white moonlight, moonlight flaked in
   rippling crescents across blue-black
      lake water just past the
   balustrade of the balcony, and they are

suspended as if in dream, their
   territory is psychic territory, dream and
      intuition's broad lunar
promontory going out over emptiness.

Others smile in ordinariness, watch the
spider-people, the fire-people, the crawling-on-all-
      fours people, the
         cow-people with absent
amusement, but they are themselves the
   rubber-people, they extend and
      stretch themselves in
all directions to please the
   pressure of all the people's expectations of them
      pulling them in all directions until
         snap-time!

Others are happy as animals, stare out as
faces stare out at us from paintings, time and
   place change, but the
      look that was painted
         into the canvas continues to
burn into the hearts of spectators centuries later!

All of these

    people and
       more at the
poetry reading, some frowning, not sure if
   disapprovingly or for
      whatever secret sudden or
        slow concern,
some close their eyes for instant transport, shadows
    lengthen under their
      chairs as they
        sail over the far planet Neptune's canyons,
others stay perfectly still and let the
news of the poems flow against their faces the same way
   they let the
     news in
newspapers flow over their
     faces, fire, famine, and
flood, people on floating house-tops
   yelling above black
       waters,
    calling across to
disaster's new neighbors.

Here in the room at the
poetry reading disaster's new
  neighbors sit
next to each other, as well as the
     new neighbors of
       ecstasy and clarity's
         release,

and I often wonder where

    people at poetry readings come from,
right out of Whitman's wheat fields wiping their
    big hands on
        overalls and
      aprons, or from the
mad hubbub of streets, just stepped off
  trolleys and subways, puzzling out their
     lives or
just longing for meaning and beauty to be as
  majestic as mountains, or out of

Garcia Lorca's patiently expectant
  wise field workers and
   students regaining their
    Moorish identity, true
      Spaniards, feeling the
       rise-up of duende's
    blackness inside them like an
oil, or from lives

filled with corporate cubicles, aluminum tubular
furniture, board meetings with
  rational purpose and
    resolution, I often wonder if the

people at poetry readings, coming out of their
  normal continuum into the
    slice of bardic intensity and then
slipping back out of it again
     into their normal continuum,
do they know about the

notebook after notebook filled with these
visions, how red-tailed hawk, osprey, cougar
   fold into the
     unfolding
       screen of the poet's poems, backyards
of circus performers perfecting their
   stunts, dedicated
environmentalists reforesting the
   rainforests with seeds out of
     leather pouches,
the living with their fire and the
dead with their cold blue faces folded like humming
  shades into the
    river of the poet's vision which these

people glimpse in passing, they themselves
fully immersed in their
   own Amazonian time-wanderings, the

items and characters of each one's life
folded slyly into their own
   panels of the
     screen, and we

face each other for a moment, space becomes
voice, past becomes
present, words float like
electrically charged feathers in the
air between us making one whole Bird of Paradise that
   hovers before dissolving, our
     momentary love-making

       dissolved into mental
          realities, heart-beat
autobiographies of God's
        constantly
     dividing and
        multiplying
           creation made
   verbal as it
was at the
    beginning, reverberating

at once through hearer and harper,
sent out from harper to hearer,

in this world made delirious by
love and its multiple lovers

dancing in pairs on the head of a

spinning

pin.

                                  3/10-11

A VEHICLE FOR THE EXPEDITIONARY IMAGINATION

While my wife sits in bed reading a novel called *"Moon Palace,"*
I sit at a table wanting to write the
   greatest poem in the world.

We have been
   staying at a motel on Highway 101 called *"The Cliff House"*
for our 10th anniversary, and I've been
reading poems to her out of my
   work in progress called *"A Maddening Disregard*
     for the Passage of Time,"
although I think of calling it by the title of
one of its poems, *"The Circular Garden."*

This has been a structured portion of time called *"the weekend"*
out of our normal routine called *"life."*

Tonight we go back home to our two children and six pets
to begin what, starting early Monday morning, is called
"the week."

I sit at a small wooden kitchen table between two
noises which seem almost the same: traffic on
Highway 101 out this little kitchenette window beside me
and the Pacific Ocean out the
open window across the bedroom in front. During the time we've been
   at this motel
it's sounded as if someone's left the water on full running in
pipes under the house, or a giant
continuous wind storm, which is

    actually the ocean. Out the
window nearer the
traffic the sound is definitely
harsher and more irregular,
    giant unseen
      trucks roaring by, as well as
          campers full of relatives.

On this little wooden table the whole
world might be summoned to appear, in this
poem called *"A Vehicle for the Expeditionary Imagination,"*
and we could travel to other
continents or other
    worlds with little
obstacle except the limitations of
    language. For poetry's both a

confrontation and an
   avoidance of reality, avoidance if we're thinking of real things like
medical insurance, paychecks and taxes, but a vehicle for
confronting deeper realities with soothing refreshment, renewal and
    fright if we're thinking of things like
  mortality and its
generous mother, immortality. Somehow we can
feel what it must be like to
    die in a poem, just as we can
sense what it is to be
more alive. In Ohio, as well as foggy Kathmandu.

Edges are illuminated wholes. The microscopic becomes
enlarged to the imaginative eye. Wing-soar and

ocean-drowning become experienced visibilities. The
   tight light of wisdom presses out
     perfect, graspable
       diamonds.
Doors open in nowhere. Saints invite us in for a
seance. We drink forbidden
    wine in its
   blessèd form. We
ride beside the great one (peace be
    upon him) on the
      wingèd donkey.

It's a matter of mental stretch and cardiac adventure
in any dusty
   corner of the world we
    happen to be in, called
"Full celebration of the life that's been so
   generously given us," or simply:

"The Rock That Won't Stop Talking."

The heart in the chest knows when it's true.

When it's not it's tacky signboards on the highway.

When it is, though, it's the tart fragrance of
   rose-gardens in the
blood, Andalusian arches overlooking patios of
   night-blooming jasmine and
  precise lute-music. Also it's
irrepressable lava flowing rapidly down from its

cone, covering hearth and steeple on its
    hot way to the sea.
It's revolution in the
    street or the
        test-tube, it's
star-flight in a
    pen-point, the wild tumbling of
people in the lit cabin of a
        space-shuttle.

Caught in my mortal body for a moment between
sound of traffic and sea-sound,
alive for the moment in a physical body, having
  thought of my personal death and then
      put it completely
        out of my mind,
my heart wants to hold out its hands
to the rest of the hearts that
    inhabit this earth, this
    fleeting imaginary world, called for a
        moment *"Moon Palace,"*
which comes into being and goes out of it again with

a sharp audible cry, and whose
    surface is as slick as
      ice in between, place of lamentation and
        indescribable joy.

Dragons and dinosaurs mingle outside the
window, grazing by the highway on ice-plant, avoiding the
  rush of traffic. We saw

    five actual dolphin-fins earlier
in the waves this morning
circling and circling, disappearing and
reappearing, participating in what is called
    "The Mating Season."

My wife reads on, occasionally
    chuckling. I
clench my teeth in the
  rush of it all, and write
    as fast as I
      can.

The event called *"Apocalypse"* is impatiently
    coming toward us
while I continue
 "A Maddening Disregard
   for the
   Passage of Time."

                                          3/11

CIRCUS VARGAS

1

The tigers' cages are wheeled out first,
  pacing striped beasts in a sea of
    children's voices and waving wands of
      cotton candy.

Ropes hang like lianas from the canvas roof,
  poles and mechanical contraptions triggered by
    pulleys, rope-ladders
     slung between
right-angled aluminum pillars.
Five cages face toward the
  center ring, man in black
    coat checking the
  latches, alert
cats pacing and looking out, pacing and
     looking out.

The lights glare, the space
is vast, enclosed in cloth,
   peaked, patchworked in angular shadows,
three rings
on the ground, red and yellow
   triangle painted. How far those
sleek beasts have come to
     arrive at this!

High-pitched animality can be heard in the

crowd's expectation.

2

The cotton candy tastes like a
soft Brillo pad dipped in stale
   strawberry Koolaid.

The spotlight swings around — the circus's
   about to begin.
Shouting hawkers, the ringmaster's
   voice with its
crisp elocutioned intonations.

First act, loud pre-taped music, the
   tigers are let out of their
cages into the
   center ring. Hang-dog, they
leap onto their pilasters.
They leap onto silvery ladders, glide through
   hoops, do a lot of
     indignities for the
  handful of tidbits he
    feeds them each time they
perform. It's a
   Rousseau jungle out there in the
center ring with
   real beasts, and a
     skinny mustachioed man in
       red satin pants gesturing

    widely with his
arms.

A tiger sits up and
   raises a paw. Another
   makes three hops on his
hindlegs. Those
   beautiful
     hindlegs! Trapped

wonderful beasts!

3

Gorgeous girls in spandex swing high on single ropes,
   men in
    sequined vests standing on the
   ground rotate them in
time to the music. Fifteen girls of
nubile age above the
    crowd keep their
bodies straight out while they hold on with
   one arm. Spiritual
athletes, they have to keep fit for this
    one moment of
     fleeting
      glory.

The high wire family with
   Latin American name, walking on

    stilts across the wire,
riding unicycles, no net
  below them,
   running backwards,
piling up impossibilities, they must be so
balanced, pure
  somehow at the
   center of their
physicality, no
   misstep allowed, no
slur of
  footing. Who are
these people? How do they
walk to the
  store for their
   groceries?

All four of them out there
  now, two walking with
poles, a platform
   between them with
    one on top and one

hanging from a
   trapeze below.

Their lives make me
   speechless.

4

The huge dusty gray elephant with the

two shapely women running around him, rubbing him,
    seems vaguely like a

  sexual metaphor, but I
can't exactly
     place it. Long trunk?
Jaunty up-curved tusks? The beast so

patiently cavorts, with its
  huge rump and
    flat feet.

At one point one of the girls, with glamorous gestures,
lies down on a red carpet in front of the
  elephant and he
    kneels on
      top of her without
   crushing her.
Elephants are in such an
outsized dimension, I've always had a
  hard time relating to their
    size, but now he

sits with huge pear-shaped back to us and looks
just like a dog sitting on its
rump. If I squint, the elephant
  looks just like

any other
small animal.

5

Of the clowns we can only
  speak of their

   irrelevance. They
divert us from the
   roustabouts taking down trapezes and nets
from the acrobatic sublime to the

grotesque-busted, platypus-footed, grimace-faced
     idiot ridiculous.

They run out after the
   high moments, they
flap around noisily then
     shuffle off in the dark
     while another act
         begins.

With tragedy always a third ingredient for the
aerialists, the acrobats, the trapeze-artists,
the clowns make poop noises,
  blow nose-trumpets,
knock each other down with
    giant rubber mallets.

The acrobats in their skin-tight suits
are ourselves,

risking our necks,
leaping out into the open air with no net,

catching and trying to
    let go,

praying for

beautiful deaths.

                                                       3/13

EXISTS!

I turn my grinning
   skull toward the light.
The night falls like a
  sheet of black
 paper over a
    needle pointing North.
Haystacks burst into flame.
Windows fill with glistening strawberries.

An owl told all the secrets of the
   parishioners to the
     fence posts and they
  fell over backwards.
One toe, grown larger than the
 others, leads all the
   rest.

It's a world made and rumpled and
  remade endlessly like a
    bed.
Its smooth covers are the air.

There are messengers on silver bicycles driving
   out of
 silver clouds with
rolled up
  messages between their
    teeth.

Gold is of
   this world, silver
   of the
   Next. O I wish all

arguments about God would
     just cease!

Exists!

                                        3/18

A MADDENING DISREGARD FOR THE PASSAGE OF TIME

Spring is
  billions of chlorophyllian carpet-weavers
    getting ready for the
      big day, and the
big day comes, and it's
  spring! They have more green thread than they
know what to do with, so they
hide it in the rolled up fabric of night so that

the next morning when you step out your door for the
first time the green
  hits you
reminding you of
  something you didn't
know you forgot. Winter is

amnesia. The body's cells conspire to
fool you. You
die in the
  winter and spring's your
    little bit of heaven. Not much. More like a
health food sandwich with
    extra sprouts. The
bread's too thick, there's
  too much tofu, and the
amount of sprouts under that
  inch slab of wheat's
    obscene. Nitrogen in the

air. Half your
   head's in
      clouds. Whole

walls could be wheeled in front of you cutting you
off from the old familiar half, while

this half enjoys sea-laps of vegetable surf slapping
   up against tumbled
      stones and winding
         paths, wildflowers in
   splatters, speckles of confettian petal-spray,

utter openness under the fierce blue gaze of
a long stretch of empty sky. Each flower a
   left-behind footprint of
      non-existent fauns, hidden inner

sexuality completely bloomed! Fragile happy petal-tissues!
Wavering just slightly in old planetary breezes!

Death a whole
   season away!

                                            3/23

SPRING RUMINATIONS

In memorium Clive (and Gene Gonder)

1

A green emerald lake spreads out at our feet
(we know by this we're in
   quasi-unreal territory.
      Scissors walk by).

On every bough of every rough-barked tree
light in star-shaped splinters spins incessantly.

From every hollow in stone or earth or wood
comes the deafening bellow that would
   cure us of our waking sleep
gentlemen, ladies, cure us of our
   chromosomal sleep that sets us to

give birth generation after generation to the
wide-eyed, the deaf-hearted, who

slide without noise into territories vacated by
   unintelligent matter. We will

slide soon enough through the screen that seems to
   shield us. Why not
 now? Tropical shapes trap us. Petal

cups in rainforest canopies filled with a
sticky fluid that both

   keeps and
dissolves us. On the surface of the glue
we see

reflections of our quizzical faces, or rather, the
   multiple reflections of a

single face. That is our
   lore.

2

I just woke up from a
   nightmare in which Satan was pressing down
heavy on my back like a large
   heavy panther digging in and
in and I began groaning and
calling out to Allah as
   hard as I could until I
woke up hearing my call out loud, anguished,
   on this side, right
here, sitting
   up now with the
     light on.

3 / Spring Aphorisms Told by a Sunlit Rock

If you comb your hair forward over a bald spot
   don't expect the wind to cooperate.

Slick ice horizontal is more fatal than slick ice vertical.

The mane of a rose doesn't make it a lion.

If stairways appeared in your mouth would those who enter descend into fetid cellars or rise into solariums of light?

Eyes reveal what words conceal.

Words conceal what the heart feels.

The heart feels what distant meadows in
   absolute solitude do at the
     break of day.

Orange sunlight in shafts of gold hit the
   heart's meadows damp with dew.

The Iron Age was human beings hammering out
    a few tools a lifetime.
  Does technology have to lead to such gluttonous excess?

The jaws of the desert open wider than the
   stomachs of forests.

Each inch of rainforest is kissed by acres of
   rainfall leaning into its green mirror.

A mist wipes away cosmetic glamour.

King Midas couldn't eat a seed, or drink a

    drop of water.

At least poverty partakes of the wisdom of the dead —
    everyone inhabits a pauper's grave at last.

The wristwatch is our personal Doomsday Book.

There's no song like the present
    that began before throats first opened
and goes on when the last ear has been sealed.

Death is Spring spelled backwards.

Spring is a sunlit rock.

4

The axe as it strikes the
    root of your evil becomes a
painted dove in triangular flight out of the sky.
Knobs of worn silver remain on
    drawers melted shut by the
        blast of your
transfigured self.
Lights in different shades and shapes on
    chandeliered shelves along
chamois walls come to
    life as you live and are lit
a thousand times brighter after your
    life goes on into

    Elsewhere.
A door outlined tight around your
shoulders first and your
   heartbeat second opens to
     let you out or
in, both hovered over
     high space, black

   pool of bright light down below.

5

A tiny pink oracle sits on a giant green branch
   and orates about spring, says
     any old thing that
comes to mind. The oracle is
   electron-microscope size, tinier than a
wavering hair, its

mouth is the air.
The air about us are its
   moving lips. The words which are like
undersides of leaves with
light coming through them
   encase us in their
     splendors.

We always walk through this half-dead
   world encased in
     splendors. A silent

branch falls on a silent
floor. Needles everywhere. Soft
   foot-falls. Of

microscopic feet. Enlarged we

see mountains as they
enter into us and take their
magisterial places on our
flats. Enlarged, we are footprints which are an

entire life printed in the air.

We pass by in a
   few turns of the seasons.
Winter extracts its cold points and we relax into

a more effortless patience.
Spring is too short to be
   comfortable in for
      long. Our

shadows elongate only to find
ourselves at this end of them
as always. I had a

friend who committed suicide this year. He's

missing this spring. Its arrival came

without him. His

eyes are lost. The

mountains don't sit inside him anymore.
Nor the seasons
    flower.

                                            3/27 (1 Ramadan) - 30

I'M STRUCK BY THE DESIRE

1

I'm struck by the desire to write a poem full of
mysterious things. I have a

longing for it — to cure the ache of mortal
incompleteness, is it that? Doors opening in

forests and letting jade green light out to
shine on the needles and branches, steam

out of nowhere which, when you
put your whole face in, you hear

voices? Haunches of large
animals, deer-like, disappearing in
fog, grindings in the night. Or

feet that appear walking, with no
body above them, at
night, or more
mysteriously, in broad
daylight. Would this bring me
closer to God? There's a

wrenching open of the chest, there's a

landscape igniting its green sparklers and
re-igniting them over and over in the

mind, these eyes made for beauty, this
heart made for truth. This mouth made for

dumb enunciations of unimaginable and
unsayable things, how

rocks got to where they are, strewing
paths and tumbled up
mountains, or the flick of

eagle-eye in space surveying the stretch below
for a nutritious twitch. There's the

constant hankering for wide-openness, as well as
tight concentration in quadrilateral

rooms, wisps of hair floating slightly above the
floor, sighs from the surrounding

emptiness. Aromas out of a
drawer. The bus stops and
opens its door, and a man with bright
green face gets out and passes
by you without
nodding. He's your
father.

You walk after him down the
street past the
others who don't
react, but he's too

swift, he's been
dead for over a
year, he disappears in a
sudden wisp. You watch

your own self
twisting like a
smoke standing
straight up from the

ground. You sense the
flatness of this
round earth rolling in

space, you catch a
glimpse in a
corner department store
window of your

green face.

2

We certainly
occupy space, but what is it that
occupies? Bones, systems churning, electric
thoughts, sexual
    stirrings, all these and
none? Our
bodies have been so

deftly created that we can be totally

oblivious to legs or buttocks, back, back of
head, toes, toe-nails, and though our

chests surround our
rib cages so
neatly, we can seem to

float suspended in
space in
rapt concentration, feeling no
boundaries to our
selves, identifying as much with immediate
wicker-chair and lace-table-clothed
table, night sounds and the
rest, until we ourselves might be mere
extensions of the
things around us into
sharp focus lit from
inside with
non-glare
lighting, sighting through consciousness
orbs, these

eyes, our hands at

work, our breath making

sound inside our
noses, the whole world flowing from our

fingertips back to

   Original Source.

3

Draw a line from our past
up past the line of trees, draw a

rhomboid from our future through the
tetrahedronal webs of interconnected

dimensions ending in
  gnat's wings or clipped
    mustache-hairs on a
 summer Sunday in Tehran, or

draw lines from now streaming actively in all
directions at terrific velocities just to keep

up with the swiftness of the present
moment which is also
perfectly still. The lines fall like floating
ribbons around life-size shapes in a
silver-walled room. Draw

lines from the deep interior, adventure and
risk, perfect equanimity and placid
resolve, concentration at the

rim of the crater in primordial
time out of which emerged all the
life forms we know today, which are a lot

less than even just yesterday, being
depleted at amazing
rates, but are a different

number certainly than way-off tomorrow's life-
forms which may be less or even
more depending on the Creator's

way with us. We cast these
bestial shadows on the wall, humans trying to be

other than they are, more
powerful than they
need be, like shrill four-footers in
elevator shoes.

Draw lines from our
actual dimensions in
time and space. Do they

lead finally to a silver ball of
twine in a high
heaven, on a
spun silver
cloud, voices like bowed

violin sonatas trilling along the

strings, hovering

eternally above the
mortal abyss?

4/1-2

SOME OF THE MYSTERIES OF THE SELF

1

I have arrived at you around a corner
   but you don't know my name,
you have fallen into me as into a pocket
    from whence you came, with a

match burning stood up on its wooden end on a
dark mahogany dresser before a
beveled mirror in Barbados just after a
monsoon. These are some of the

vital mysteries of the self.

A man in sequined tights, with
   wife and children, puts his
head way inside a lion's mouth. The
lion also has wife and children, and isn't used to having
a man's head put so far inside its
mouth.

The mysteries of the self in the dark, lying
naked and spread-legged on a low cot listening
to the wind. Feeling neither

fear nor certainty, but being more a mere
extension of the furniture, an
aspect of the walls, a short
melody heard in passing in the more

grandiose symphony of the wind.

Fragmentary mysteries of the self. Draped on
antlers. Crouched under a
table. In the
back of a vegetable truck crossing the Alps,
uncomfortable for six straight hours on
gunny sacks of potatoes on the way to
violent revolution and death by a
chest wound that bled and bled.

Mortal mysteries of the self. Your
last thoughts about a green childhood
bicycle you left out in the rain. Against a
   green wall, the
   exact same
     shade of green.
Wipeout Polaroid mental obsessive snapshot
mystery of the self in its
     dissolve. Or

under a bridge of bright blue mist near a
roaring waterfall after
eight days of concentration on the
Creator's manifest mysteries, a shout like a

shot and you're
gone but the
  mist remains.

Mysteries of the self turned inside-out like a

silk handkerchief used to wipe the
sweat off a woman in labor in
Mongolia in which another
human self is born to icy snow for miles, ice and
snow and incessant blizzards, and be named
for a dead great uncle and live to
ripe manhood in red jacket and
black pointed cap and marry Myshrinka of the warbling throat
who sings in the smoky vestry with a voice
   makes everyone cry.
What mysteries of the self! No

end to them, seasonal they
turn, out of
season they plunge like anti-gravitational

meteors to some other
planetary system entirely, wear

God's Face for a single moment but
won't say they did. I

submit without a struggle to the
implacable mysteries of the
  self.

2

The self is only too eager to drink
  milk of Paradise, only too

eager to lie down with
    Lamb of God,
to catch sight of the radiant virgin taking her
  stroll through the
    rude rocks, the self is only too

prone to lose itself in a room of smoky laughter
or press against the lizard's belly
   under a full moon.

If it were not a mystery there would be no
movement. Steps toward perfection would
never be taken. The
grease of afterbirth would
  cling forever to our skin. But like the
young buck's rubbing of moss off his growing
antlers on the rough bark of trees

the self rubs its own skin raw to reach
true growth underneath.

Swimming in emerald waters, heat-glow and
  shimmering lights both
    within and above the
      pool, the self has stepped down
among the first lepers to be
   healed. The
self knows the score. Can look the
  healer in the eyes and not
    shrink from the
seismic traction of change. Old

    crusts shaken away, plate
      glass crashing from the
        fortieth floor onto the
          street.

Like a lake of membranous silk the self expands to be
watering hole for
    stray beasts that pass.
      Washing place for the
larger quadrupeds. Can be

light on the surface of a pearl, or
the pearl itself on the throat of a young beauty
    with skin like shimmering milk.

Ladders of self step out of the self onto
selfless surfaces. There is in the self

a cure for the self's ills. The thing that is
killing it, turned, can become its
relief. In the pit of its own

depth, breath of summer flutes and bee-hive
    symphony can wrap around its
  middle like a rope and pull it
      up from its drowning.

And when

white wind comes rolling down from
Parenthesis Peak, out of

    space that is not
      space and
time that moves neither
  forward nor backward, but
    only from side to side, all the

ghost's illusionary rags float off self's fragile frame,
dissolve like paper in flame or
the annoyance of seasonal bugs, summer's
    fleas perishing in
    winter's cold. What was so

urgently solid and passionately stirred for a
flash or a lifetime flutters like flags of
surrender before
    flying away, revealing themselves to have

had no real substance at all, ever, in the
sound of celestial hooves passing over self's
rush of immaterial clouds

casting only the thinnest of running shadows
down below on self's
basking dunes.

3

Or the self is like an organic
    radio receiver getting signals from the
      highest mountain peak in any

   planetary system, its
mechanism made of natural things, silky
honey-comb, tendril, subtle
   vegetable twine triggers and hair-thin switches,
    the inevitable
   perfectly geometrical crystal, and it

picks up the signals loud and clear as long as the
mechanism's clean, positioned properly, plugged
   in, well-oiled and in generally good

working order.

4

Having sung once, the singer
   wants to
    sing again. That's
one of the mysteries of the
    self.

The self sits in a corner in a house of
white mist with all its
windows open, and a
   sheer white wind blows in from all
directions at once to the center, accompanied by a shrill
   whistling sound, the self

sits in a chair in the corner like particles of
memory attached to a stiff broomstick, haunted and

minimal, stripped of its subtle technological
pretensions. If a

personage of indefinite shape but with eyes like
fiery beacons could

come to each one of us privately sometime in our
tattered lives and pin the
badge of sainthood-achieved-against-all-odds on our breasts
it would be pleasantly convenient. Or if at least

the red slime of sinfulness were wrapped like
Christmas ribbon around our ghastly and
corpulent forms with their
glistening worm-like lips of despicable sensuality then

everything would at least be as
clear as a bell, we'd
all know our places, like
wooden statue mastheads on
prows of ships we could cut
proudly into death. But reality isn't so

neat. It's one of the
endless mysteries of the
self that the

saintly one in life may have a
secret splotch so great it
chains him by the neck and heart, and the
corpulent sinner may shed tears in

earnest over injustice or
someone's battered
spirit and the gates of
chiming glass swing
open like the
waters of the Niagara to let that

person's whole being in onto
escalators of sound so rare no
earthly instrument can
come close to sound it. One of the

sphinx-like mysteries of the
self is that we
never know, while the
earthly jazz-band tootles and jams, so

subtle are its machinations, the self's wild
swings from zenith to nadir and nadir to zenith again like
forked lightning over the
sea at night, and

wind comes in all the open windows at
once in the self's mysterious house of mist to
brush our faces with its
rivers of quickly vanishing script.

5

The alchemist bent forward in lifelong concentration, so

carefully repeating the experiment, face
blackened from the soot of former explosions,
patiently reconstructs the steps of red
powder, solar dust, white mud, emerald
potions, golden smoke.

Darwin with his notebook, looking lizards in the
eyes no civilized man had stared
into before, time smashing time as the
Nineteenth Century crashed into prehistory, in his
frock-coat investigating reality for himself,
leaning way out over the edge of the Impossible.

The face of the self of mankind is filled with the
first light of awe each time it
dawns again, brought

back to the pristine timelessness that actually
ticks in silken twitches through this
universe of time, a

colorless light spread along our
cheeks, seeping in through our
eyes and down
electric spines to our

hearts where mountains actually
move aside to let the
pure first and last light
of creation enter there.

6

If I should die tonight, the self is

all the attempts we made to know, only to
come up against not knowing, like a
rose arbor filled with roses reflected by a
pool of clear water in the center.

The self is a blue farmhouse on a green hill under a
    black sky, three white
  horses swish their tails as they
        graze nearby,

the self is ten-story libraries with
archives three stories underground connected by a
spiral staircase watched over by a
blind Argentinean librarian.

The self is the universe in ten stories above ground and
three below inside the
blind Argentinean librarian, he
    gazes at himself in a mirror and sees back
      rose arbors reflected in
         still pools.

The self is a swallow with a bent wing, a taxi with
flat tire, an elevator
    plummeting to the ground, an
      airplane landing on the
        alps while the

passengers write last thoughts on their
place-mats and tuck them into their
    briefcases to be
        discovered in the
           charred wreckage.

The self is a lobster on a string walked down the
   avenue by a visionary who sees a face
more beautiful than Beatrice roll through
    alpine clouds like a halved moon, smile
   more infinite than
        time and number, softer than
           deep death.

The self is black next to white, criminal next to
   cardinal in a small rowboat in the Azores —

if I should
die in my sleep tonight, the self is
yellow parrots slyly exotic among giant green foliage,

a letter written, crossed out and
rewritten, then sealed with a wax seal that says
"He who sets out surely arrives. Embark at once!"

The self is lazy frilled skins pulled tight around an
empty core, onion only edible when
    cooked.

The self is hundreds of unused stairways, miles of
untaken roads, acres of unplowed fields and

one handle which, when found and
    grasped, transforms

all the rest.

7

The self sang a few sad songs
    then dissolved away.
Oh, and it was a
    sad sight to see.

Through the spokes of the
   turning wheel you could
     see it dissolve to the
strains of its somber, self-pitying
    music. Menhirs on the
      plain, tall standing
rocks against howling North winds
   toppled like toothpicks. The self
of each sweet individual creature of us, each
   winsome pack of trouble with
     occasional relief, each
individuated hierarchy of staunchly defended
  opinions and personally skewed
     interpretations of events and their
       meanings, interpretations of
interpretations by a one-sighted, turf-paranoid
interpreter who only speaks
half the original language, the other half

vouchsafed by angels.

The self is our
burden and our
boon. Angels have no
self. They are

obedient light who move as waves move, as
particles dancing in a
light-beam on their anti-gravitational
errands.

But with these wondrously gaseous-balloon-blown-up
selves we've got from birth onwards, we have a

chance to let wings from obtuse territories
engage with the clumsy machinery of our
usual selves and suddenly

disappear from their own cognition, go out
vertical trap-doors into spatial exuberances in which no

vestige of those soiled selves remains but only
traced outlines set up on the
plains like those
menhirs through whose now great empty spaces

the soul, unencumbered of self, flies
directly to God.

4/3-6

TRANSFORMATIONS

The lynx looked into a mirror and saw
   a pussycat.
A lion went through a door and became
   a god
      in the eyes of the villagers whose
children were at risk.
The turtle is in no hurry, though dragonflies
   hover before zipping away.

Do the images of people on downtown streets that pass
before plate-glass department store show-windows
     remain etched in the molecular memories of
        the glass?
Everything stops for a split second before
   carrying on. Stops

again in mid-track. Clicks ahead.
A grin becomes tragic mask surrounded by
     red smoke. Yellow

fills the air and we're back to balloons.
Trees' round leafy tops blow like Afro-hair on the
   slopes of a dark green knoll.
Butterflies don't even remember being fuzzy worms.
They don't regret the lack of so many sticky feet.
Or if they do, when they see their
   reflections on the
     surfaces of lakes do they
       pause and

    wonder in awe at the
        incomparable beauty of change, or do they

fly on oblivious to the depths of such
uncanny philosophy?

The old man who dies on the first day of Spring
brings a certain winter collage element of
    unrenewable cold to that
        brightest of long days. He

travels on, clad in new shoes, ice-blue with gold laces
radiating a seasonless light. He skims over

waves and particles practicing mimicry in a time-band
through rippling curvatures of space. He gives them

a wink and a nod and sails on, happy as the
butterfly and as glad to be free of

feet at last in his new terrain. Clouds also

shift and change endlessly, shadow and break open
to let slanting sun-rays enter.

A pearl emerges from the soft wet glands of an oyster,
hard result of an
    unavoidable irritation in
time. We will all wear

bright new faces on the other side, some bright with the

newly revealed darkness of the abyss they've been in for so long
calling out in unaccustomed voices of prayer, having
totally lost facial expressions of
    pride and self-adoration,

faced with the nitty-gritty of a

Face beyond question, pure

Face beyond human description.

Truly

naked at last.

                                                               4/8

BAD DREAM

In my dream, what must have been
   going on was that I
 told the suicide to
    prove he was still alive, and he
apparently did, or at least there was a
change in the air. I was turned to the
wall, and suddenly I was
desperate and began calling
out to Allah, *"Allah! Allah!"* but

couldn't turn around, couldn't
face my invisible or visible assailant, kept
calling desperately out, then *"Oh Allah please
help me,"* over and
over, but it

gave me no comfort. I couldn't
turn around and I
couldn't wake up, so I

renewed my efforts, must've
filled the house with my

actual audible cries, until finally I
woke myself up in the
same position as in the

dream, tingling all over, hearing my
   voice in my ears, wondering just how

full of fear I must be after all
who think myself fearless, but

calling out to
Allah pulled me
through, Allah

pulled me
totally through.

                                                                                            4/8

THE EYES

I wanted to write a poem this afternoon about the
   flash of the eye, the
     incomparable miracle of the live
        glisten of the human eye, this

afternoon at the ball park watching my
twelve-year old son play
baseball, I noticed
young eyes flash and
   glisten with light and
     life as the
       air grew
   that brownish soft
dark of the
   setting sun, I just

remembered it now past
midnight trying to remove
   an eyelash in the mirror, when you really
look yourself searchingly in the
   eye hunting for the source of the
annoyance, and how

when someone is faced away from you, in
profile, they are still anonymous, but when you see their
eyes, or make actual
eye-contact, a person assumes sympathetic
   personhood,
eternal uniqueness has been

displayed the way a
   traveling merchant might display rare
diamonds against a dark velvet
     case, something

rare glistens in the eye, a visual hollow that goes
right to the soul, you get the
   unvarnished truth no matter what the
     lips underneath them are
       saying.

Eyes don't lie, or only at
terrific expense, veiling them is so
   difficult, if we could only trust what we

see eye to eye!

The blind retain their anonymity because they can't make
that all-revealing contact, they are a
  people unto themselves, like the
    Sufis in the Moroccan desert I spent the
      afternoon with on a sun-drenched
        rooftop terrace, out of
twenty only about five of them could
see, yet they carried on as if they all could,
singing,
   laughing,
     drinking mint tea, kidding each other, playing
       jokes, bursting into
Qur'an recitation, singing
   ecstatically again, silent, sipping their sweet mint

tea and laughing — what
   joyous company! Then, when we had
gone downstairs at dusk, a
prince of Sufis came into the
room, a poor black man of statuesque
beauty in a pure white
djellaba of the desert, he sat down with
noble dignity and began to
recite the Qur'an to break your heart, and the
   others all
     wept, and
he too was blind, and to this

day they all seemed a
people unto themselves
   in a high citadel close to the
clouds, they walk on the
earth, but aren't
a part of its weirdness, their

visual doors open inward. But the

flashing eyes of the sighted of us
open outward, each to
each, across even
distances, are like a
confession of instant recognized love, an
invisible embrace, a silent unanimous

witness to our collective
humanhood, all

seeing what we
   see from our
  various vantages, maybe from the
    same silver pool of glistening
  innocence, primordial
    freshness,

soft gelatinous orbs in
  sockets of hard bone that burn with
passionate fire, cut with icy
intellectual glare, melt with
   heart's compassion, say

what can't be
said, are the

opened-up soul-window of a person in their
face of what is hint and
revelation of each of our

secrets from first light before birth to

past the
darkening lid drawn-down
absolute end

of this visible world.

                                                                        4/10

LANDSCAPES COME IN DIFFERENT SIZES

for David Federman

Landscapes come in different sizes.
The Grand Canyon (rust gulches, blue sunlight)
is not the same as our front yard parched with drought.
Rocks come in different shapes, inhabit different
  dimensions from each other. Shadows

can be worn straight or at angles. Light

can't resist getting into everything, or
wholeheartedly embracing the light "from within," causing
major electrical storms over huddled farmhouses in
  Kansas, that
    flat golden tablecloth under a
      flung gray sky. *"Well, that about*

sums it up," the Dimension-Architect said, rolling up
a universe, some of it
  spilling back out to create
    tiny inhabited worlds. Speech also

has weight, duration, pitch and speed. Leaves
traces. Holes. Wells. Blights. Beautifies better than

four hour mud-bath treatments, turns ugly faster than
a fascist invasion of people trying to
  mind their own business of coming to
    premature birth and dying

way past their prime. Droplets of ice fall

on oxidized tabletops left out all year.
People fill the square in woolen overcoats to coach
village chess players who play with life-sized pieces.
The rain reaches the stone lion's paws. He

does not flinch. Februaries don't fit into

anyone's pocket. It's a wild card month in a
wild card season. Anything could

happen, and does. Winter looks good tucked there

behind your ear. Wear your

heart on your sleeve and you could conduct

the orchestra of the world.

4/13

ICE-SWANS

for Malika

The future's as bright as the
  eye that beholds it. The

past's as dark as the eye that
  shuts down its revisionist lids over what was,
in all its
    fluted subterfuges. Now the

present's another matter altogether. We're always going
on and on about the present, *the*
  present this, the present that, be
    totally in the
present, the
 now is
  all there is, whereas in fact the

present doesn't exist. As
  soon as it's
    passed our
      lips, it's past. We are a

momentary opacity before
  eternity's transparency. So much light getting
through sculpts us like a
    chef sculpts ice-swans just before the

banquet, but as soon as a
  form has fully emerged, or even a
little bit before, it starts

to melt. When the
   evening's over, a cold
      puddle's all that
         remains.
Forms disintegrate at the
peak of their perfection. Elderly

   couples waltz and
      fox-trot around it, beads of
         icy sweat roll down
      rounded wings, the
         fox-trotters also
            fluttering insubstantially before the

greater movement of the
   stars. A

larger dimension always
   engulfs us. No

need to cry out. The

demons have all
turned to butterflies. See, there they

go above the blazing farmhouse. Twilight catches

the falling
powder of their
wings.

                                                                                  4/14

CUT A TREE

Cut a tree, make a matchstick
burns forests to the ground.

Cut a tree, make a book
talks about deforestation.

Cut a tree, make a toothpick
corporate developer uses to clean his teeth.

This notebook I write in
was a flourishing tree.

May my words ring true.

4/16

THEME AND VARIATION

I guess if you were to pinpoint the theme and
    variation of my work you might say it's

the creative imagination entering into
being and drawing close
around bright perception highly
inhabited worlds — in the

middle of this defunct society of
    desperation, the absolute inability to imagine

a universe without God. Golden

  pods like sentient
    bubbles on the
      ends of stems
sing the same song. Perfection of
    hook-hairs in
        symmetrical rows along
feathers make the
    same claim. If it's a

barren salt desert in
    all directions, something in it casts

  pale blue shadow, and that
    shadow alone attests to the
live existence of God. God casts no

shadow, but
   without God no
      shadow is
         cast.

Woolly protuberances everywhere we
   look, lapis lazuli beads along the
edges of knife-blades, worlds of
geometric order in the
      sub-microscopic realm I'm never tired of
singing, all
   reflect back the
      impossibility of
order without an
      Orderer, an

Ordainer. Ordinary

wonder. *Uh-huh.* Bland as

paint. Sea-wall
flaked by wind. Those
insistent waves. Invisible

troubadours of changes in the daily weather, rhyming
with difficult rhyme all
   existence with its
interior-most essence. Tree-frogs

blink, being
   completely themselves. They enter into the

picture by the
  sheer fact of their
    being. Their

green glisten means
  nothing beyond
    itself, but that

itself is all, that
  itself is totally

enough to knock the hats off stuffy

arguers from here to Prague in the Kafkian
  winter of '89, before the

  waltz-music in the

bandstand behind the

blinding white
  eruption
    struck up.

4/17

WILL WE HAVE TO INVENT OUR OWN FOREST OF TREES?

1

Will we have to invent our own
   forest of trees, O God, our own

clear-water lakes reflecting back upside down in
   rippling spindly black
the pine-trees lining them? The peaceful
ivory pavilion, match-light to light up
iron lanterns on hooks, a little
   orange light inside the
      forest deeps with a
bright day-blue sky above it all, as in a
painting by Magritte? Will we be

forced to eat what we ourselves have
made of this earth, or will You bring it all

back for us? Could we be
turned completely around in ourselves to face
renewal on our own?

To shave our
excesses back to the bone,
the shining white sentinels of our assembled
bones, semaphores on a
   dark horizon to generations yet
      unborn?

2

Maybe we've tried to
   disinvent it, Lord, take the whole thing
down tack by tack, atom by
     atom, to fly the
threads that hold life together in the
   air like tentative webs looking for a
        new landing ledge. We've tried to

draw up out of life's bowels everything useful to make our
   machinery run — we'll

suck it dry to make our
   machinery run! We've

put our faces flat down onto its grate to
scare it into submission, Bikini Island, un-
    inhabitable now, Chernobyl, ghost-town of a
        thriving city, dead
          electric wires like
        tightropes whose tightrope
          walkers have all
fallen to their deaths during the
        Saturday matinee.

We tear into her with childish eagerness.
We're too
   sophisticated now to have to approach the
      earth with anything like
         reverence...

3

When we
  reduce the universe to a
    sigh or
      wisp of smoke
twisting above a formica tabletop in a
     lab, we still find ourselves
gazing at a
  reflection of
    ourselves. Wave of green

light in the
  air above the tabletop, emerald-flecked
suds of light broiling froth from
eternity to eternity in the

darkened lab after hours, droplets of original
matter forming on the inside of the
  outside, and all along the
    rim of the
      rimless, but one single

real seed in the belly of its
sprouting has all the
quintillions of creation's

live energies within it to prove beyond the
power of doubt the

    resiliency of blooms that go

even past the death of nuclear rooms.

Even past the
death of nuclear rooms.

                                            4/19 - 25

WHY DOES THE SOUL LOVE POETRY?

1

Out of all possibility,
  why does the soul love
    poetry? Why does a jet of black
     spout up from
  depths usually ignored?

At the sound of words precisely placed, at the
rub of sonorous edges, reverberations that
dislodge something usually asleep?

Rubies glimmer in drab cinder block walls,
dragonfly wings scintillate their
    oil and water shimmer. Dusk has
fallen and people have become more serious,
the night is coming on and laughter has become more
thoughtful with the coming dark.

Birds are still. Eyes are closed. Shutters also.
Hearts are opening.

2

A lone singer on a stone
  leaves his throat open to
    deepest breezes.
In his eyes hurt catches fire, longings

conflagrate. Voices from distant horizons
gather and become visible. Dark-maned

horses are churning in white-flecked sea-surf.
No silence for miles around. All the elements

pour through the singer's song.
Even the stone he sits on
   begins to long for its
      geological home.

3

Element of the elements, the soul
  has ears for what
our usual flat daily cycles
    cannot satisfy. Where eyes see

straight boulevards, high-rise buildings,
plate-glass consistencies, the soul in its
  glowing grotto moves toward the
    magnet of earth's deepest groans,

flying fireflies of the divine lightness of being, of

stars drunk in their starry deeps, and the soul

shakes off its millennial sleep and
rises perceptibly to greet them. Above the

human clearing — mortal bodies moving around in the half-light down below — the song-drenched

soul begins to flow upward.

4/26

WHERE DOES IT ALL COME FROM?

Where does it all
  come from? Where does it all
go? If I put my hand in a
    rent in the cloud will I
      draw out
  goose of gold or egg of solid sound?

When the
  heart is set in motion,
    miracles occur.
A window walks along the street through which we
can see ourselves
  walk along the street. Trees
flower unexpectedly. Mothers and fathers appear
   beaming in doorways, drying their hands along the
    sides of their clothes, greeting us with the
same enlightened gazes they use to
bid us farewell. Waterfalls

sit high up on their
  haunches before
    splashing completely down. The heart's
canoe rides frothing
  rapids to the
    placid lake where
     storks on
       one leg preen

folding wings.

Where does all this come from,
    heavenly patchwork of
      images and
        ideas sewn so
tenuously together? And when the
slight wind blows, or the
    great wind like a
      camel's eyelid closing
        down against sand-storm,
bas-reliefs on ancient walls come alive and the
    figures walk right off them and get

lost in the crowd, ancient
stiff-backed Babylonians among Californians
    lazily shopping for
      flip-flops,

does the same source supply
enraged fanatics with bad breath and just causes
as the silver sickle moon that might hang for a
    split second over this poem?

Does the same gate open into a garden as into
a room of domestic disaster, the
    estranged husband home from the
      factory with a
        sawed-off shotgun?

Do the same breezes carry songs as well as
    cries?

Does a warm darkness cover all, or a
chill blue comforting light? Choirs among
   cloud-chairs, tipped on their
     front legs ascending
       silvery beams of
         chill blue light?

Is the rumble of tank-tread the same as a
single bureaucrat clearing his throat?

Where does it all
come from, the
intake of breath, by bird or
   potentate, and when

sail-tops disappear below the horizon just after
   catching fire, and the

iron and marble stairways go straight up to an
iron and marble blank wall instead of a
   doorway, do the

lovers whose entwined arms make a
jump rope of silent music, the
   steam of their beings encompassing
    elephants
      two-by-two up the
       ramp to the
        ark,
do they go with the going of great
   civilizations, a

    whirling bell left on a
      rafter tinkling very
tinily in the tiniest of
   breezes? And the
marching heavenly shadows on the
wall, do they go there
  too, stoppered in a
    transparent
      bottle on a
    celestial
      tabletop?

Music and thoughts, embodied in
physical bodies, coming into
happy existence and going right
  out of it again, leaving
    hardly any
      residue, will they
all come together into a giant comprehensible
  pattern, or will we

sit in a blue wind with crystal
  tears in our eyes in the
    last doorway praising the

Origin of all origins, the Source of all
  sources and the
final End of all

ultimate final ends?

                                                5/2

SWIRL

The swirl in our coffee cups nearly jumps
  out of the cup and
    spins in the
      air, but doesn't.
It's all a sensitive chaos, bridges of
  bright light leaping all by
    themselves over the
      flood. Mustaches keep
growing even on the most
undeserving hoodlum. The old woman in the
back room sitting in her
  rayon slip with her
    nylons rolled
      down around her
ankles has just been crowned
Queen of the Netherlands in her
  imagination, and her
plastic curlers almost
    glitter in the glare. Whole

islands worth of dust fall down around the
modern metropolis, city planners at
giant dry-marker boards in cavernous
board-rooms dictate the directions and cloverleaf
intersections worth millions of
  dollars of high-tech construction, while

unseen on green stems, on rosebushes lining the courtyard,
    lighter green

aphids get deliciously milked, make little
audible munching sounds as they
   chew and look back with soft beady
     eyes at their busy
       milkers.

A swirl of light over Los Angeles, in the eye of the
beholder, in the
   corner of an
     ornate mirror, in the
heart of the newly illumined, takes us

all by surprise. Goes by

unnoticed by cab-driver mentalities who want only to
   get through the
thickest traffic in the
     shortest time.
A lovely velvety flood of soft blue surf crawls
   elegantly along the
     shoreline.
We have that
   loveliness inside
     us. Sexual chaos is

resolved when we
   lie back relieved and
enlivened. We rode the

waves of the lengthening
   swirl as it

rose from our
    coffee cups. Our body's waves

flooded the
    usual boundaries. One glimpse
        was all we had of a
silver crescent over your
bare shoulder, above the

ghostly matchstick houses, saliva-thread perfect shacks
        spiders build to
            stay the
    night in. Gone by
morning.

We are all
    gone by
morning. But what
    licks of
        swirl the tongue finds still fresh at the

corners of our
    lips! What

recurrences! Our hearts delight
    in the swirls of these

resonating
    occurrences!

5/4

BEETLES

The thing about beetles is:
wherever they land
they keep on walking.

5/4

THE DEEPEST GROUND

My latest writing desk is a
  large square flatish book
called: *"The Great King... King of Assyria,"*
Metropolitan Museum of Art publication showing the
    bas reliefs in their
      collection, and to see these
flat figures with Assyrian eyes and noses doing their
almost two-dimensional dance along the flat surface of those
ancient walls sets me
  going in the dark directions of
    poetry, to fall into crumbling dust, let my
borders and their
  border-guards down, follow the
    slow or swift drift to the
Ground, with a
capital "G", sink into the

Assyrian Ground of anonymous being to re-arrive among
talkative columns overlooking a clear blue sea,
talk among those columns with the
  long-dead, see through their
    almond eyes, have their
      slightly curled smiles like taut
    bows in the hands of master
      archers, those
curled beards like fluted
  columns themselves, or like the
Rastafarian heads of ropey black hair in our
    own time, sound of

    sistrum, O
       sound the
         sistrum and bring out the
           dancers, we're going to
crumble through the
       dust of all
         dissolutions and re-
emerge long dead and already ancient to walk along the
shoreline and call out with no
       voice but
         majestic echoes that come curling

all the way up into the
late twentieth century to
     rattle among
      subway cars, fly
up against the
labyrinthine walls of our
        overpopulated cities

to see if anything at all, any of those cries
   that arise out of the
deepest Ground of our
   beings, can be

heard.

                                 5/5

HOUSE FRONTS

1

Accordions of house fronts open up and there are
   faces on each one, doors for
      mouths, windows eyes, roof hair
         shaped distinctively as the
house fronts jumble up rickety streets, and
voices from each one begin
   whispering along the line, passing

messages of humanity from house to house, lights
   go on, shades go up, lights go
     off, shades get drawn, one house
       shouts in pain, one cries out in
         hopelessness, one grins and starts
tittering, one
laughs out loud, one begins this

lengthy monologue, recounting children and grandchildren,
the blind nephew, the lame dowager aunt, grand-
   parents all the way
     back to Methuselah, hunchbacked great-great
grand-father the genius navigator, hopping among
swiftly uncoiling ropes over the Seven Seas in search of
Polish treasure, cross-eyed great-great aunt Du Barry, from
   noble lineage, whose
     elegant neural twists were the
       results of close intermarriage, whose
   compassion for small creatures was

    legendary, who single-handedly inaugurated the
first Humane Society in Varburg, 1872, or

the first Nursing Home for Ailing Theatrical Performers, 1863,
or back even further, to
    Nestor of Enchilnarsus, from actual
gladiator stock, broke twelve
      iron chains with his bare hands, smashed twelve
human adversaries, lived to be 93 (unheard of
then), married seven times, his
   male children all became
     senators, his female children all became
  senators' wives, one concocted the first
cough medicine, or back further still, through low-lying

bands of bright green mist over the
    marshes, we're getting out of

touch with recorded history here, but the
links are still strong, now the women are more
memorable, their wisdom connects with what's
appropriate for each
season, one named approximately
    Glarhelda splits the first
      seed-case, activates one of the first of
        several domesticated
   melon-patches, is

sought out for her
deep knowledge, was
buried sitting

up among twisting
golden vines.

Now we shoot
forward through
   several branches of
labyrinthine genealogies right past the accordioning

house fronts of
   ourselves past our
own children's grandchildren to the

future race who knows no horses,
populations who have lost most of their
language, who
   communicate telepathically, in visual
test patterns and
swirling snow-pictures, overly tall and
nuclearly irradiated ones, with
   strange transmutations, ones whose

deformities have created extra-sensory
   capabilities, one who developed

two mouths, spoke parallel
   comprehensible sentences, one with

tremendous brain who could transport whole
block-loads of specially outfitted citizens to
other planets through the power of
thought alone — might these not actually already

exist in our human molecules, might these
time-warriors, quantum leapers,
apocalypse survivors, actually

show their super-humanly beautiful faces to us
through unclear, then clear
   window-like corrugations in
     time and space, with their
heavy and
sensual eyelids, their
  still but
     beautifully formed

tremendously tender
   lips?

2

Out of one house a
  particular figure comes
spangled in sun-rays, the
   genius of all the rest. Dazzling blue
outline, face of rampant silver, rapid slivers of
   lightning tiny as ink-dots, jaggedly

splendid cheetah-movements, this figure, naked as
new snow, glistens through the
dark air, and is the

emblematic embryonic potential grace emerged from

all the rest, their
   uttermost
      perfection, walking
   sturdily on
splayed light-beams, stepping
suddenly into the
great air of pine forests, pungent
   scent that
      ignites our
   dead senses, they

wake up like souls out of
   tombs, sit up and embrace in their
      tight harmony this

figure whose wingless human
singleness gives
   rise to
      melodious song.

3

Is it the deliciously gorgeous eternity implied in
   nights filled with crickets that makes them so
liberating, the whole soul
   floats edgelessly through Amazon lengths of
      night when it's filled with natural
         creature cries, corridors of

life-connection, insinuating a

     natural before and a continuous
    after to the present moment the soul so
longs for, I so
   long for suddenly having been
     reminded of it by a piece of modern music that
uses recorded animal sounds and ends with continuous
      cricket thatch. I was

suddenly in Nigeria. My
one year there, how hard by day, hot and airless,
    but how sweet the
  nights, they seemed so long and so
     God-blessed, so much

nocturnal life come awake, the ship of our days like a
huge dark lozenge going slowly down an even huger canal of
greater darkness, stars, earth under us, space all
  around us, with
    small animals coming out, calling to
      each other, subtle on
  soft paws, unseen nose-twitch, unseen
     seeing eyes, tongues, hunting,
love-making, just

noisily existing in their melodious animal ambience,
that totally haunting down-scale bird-song of
   nostalgic nuance, every night, like a
     xylophone of poignant longing, me now also totally

longing for a corridor of primal nature around me,
water-sound, night-sound, gone from me almost

completely here in the city, except for occasional cat-yowl —

will it become

gone from the

earth forever? O

man bereft? O most poignant

lonely soul?

                                                           5/12 -14

FIRST TEACHER, LAST TEACHER

My first teacher was a
  rock on a
sandy plain who
  turned into a crowded
    grocery during the
      full moon.
My parents were raindrops, falling hand in
  hand onto the
    rock. I was
born in wedlock. My first

playmates were gusts of icy wind,
they'd come
  racing around
    corners on their
way to the
  track of time. I lost all

track of time. I was

wedded myself to my first wife who was

a wine, a rose dipped in
  tar, topaz in
    mud, rooftop over
lava, delivered
  of larva, loved in
laughter and
  left ajar. Love was so

livid, flies could
   walk its edge, flowers

live on its ledge. Don't ever

leave me alone. I was

once left alone.

I died and was
   lowered into the
      land. Rock was my

first teacher, my
   last teacher
      sand. At the

side of my tomb I see
my children dry-eyed and the
   world wet-eyed, or
 vice-versa. I have left a

legacy of a lover's

light-lined
nothingness. Let a

single line of singing
   sound lie
     awake in its
rough somethingness!

TIME

> "Do not curse time, for time is Allah."
> — *Hadith of the Prophet (peace be upon him)*

What are the times of day?

Why do they arrive with such
   regularity? After the

volcano's erupted and covered the
   entire village with hot red mush

noon arrives, somewhere people stop to lunch, someone
puts his rowboat out onto a lake. Night falls.
Light plays eerie ripples on the hardening
   igneous ash. Moonlight at midnight. And

the dawn. A

ball rolling across sky's billiard table, with the
cue of the sun striking it from its
   pivotal location. Morning

comes, ladders, buckets, brief-cases and binders
bundled up and trundled
   out back doors, as we

put our soul's plow-wedge against the onslaught apocalyptic
   regularity of the
hours of the day. Accomplishment makes the

happy Taoist carefully fold his sleeves.

Lack of accomplishment makes the organic interior
gastric battlefield fill with toxic juices, wavy
parachutes baling out of planes twisting like
   fluffs of burning
      dandelion down a
         bleak sky.

Light still slants on the rolling ball
  no matter what. The hours come on time. After
    car wreck, after
ambulance and vigil, late morning arrives,
noon, late afternoon. Soon nightfall sews its
    stretched black
edges into the corners of our living rooms.

Patients are wheeled down white hallways.

In some places it's always night. Mine-shafts,
prisons, hospitals. Windows fill with
full-color pictures, but it's
Divine Light greater than
the heroic figures in the
  stars twenty-four hours that gives each
     moment its microscopically
   detailed drama, fragments of
      epic dialog bouncing above the
        clatter of metal wagons.

Lunchtime comes even after we die. One less at the table.

The dawn comes bright and early, and the night
goes by in the diminishing sounds of car traffic
    down Milpas Street.

As I write this poem in
  real time, the future is not yet
    created, the future a great
      white tunnel the
        size of time, but

parallel sprocket-tracks already
in place for it to run on.

Umbrellas in our hearts are already
up for strong rainfall. Left and right gloves are already
  twisted together in
anxious anticipation.
Glass doors are already cleansed of any
smudges to let next day's sunlight, noon-light,
    or twilight in

to set
slanted dust-filled bright perpendiculars
on the stacked
  furniture of our

exact presences.

Time moves into us like boisterous tenants into rapidly
deteriorating buildings. Deep shadows fill noisy stairwells.

Time washes our bodies in poignant candid photographs
of actions made once then
completely forgotten.

Time arrives on schedule with perfect regularity,

looks deep into our faces. Finds us

just as we are.

5/20

ABOUT THE AUTHOR

Born in 1940 in Oakland, California, Daniel Abdal-Hayy Moore's first book of poems, *Dawn Visions*, was published by Lawrence Ferlinghetti of City Lights Books, San Francisco, in 1964, and the second in 1972, *Burnt Heart/Ode to the War Dead*. He created and directed *The Floating Lotus Magic Opera Company* in Berkeley, California in the late 60s, and presented two major productions, *The Walls Are Running Blood*, and *Bliss Apocalypse*. He became a Sufi Muslim in 1970, performed the Hajj in 1972, and lived and traveled throughout Morocco, Spain, Algeria and Nigeria, landing in California and publishing *The Desert is the Only Way Out*, and *Chronicles of Akhira* in the early 80s (Zilzal Press). Residing in Philadelphia since 1990, in 1996 he published *The Ramadan Sonnets* (Jusoor/City Lights), and in 2002, T*he Blind Beekeeper* (Jusoor/Syracuse University Press). He has been the major editor for a number of works, including *The Burdah* of Shaykh Busiri, translated by Shaykh Hamza Yusuf, and the poetry of Palestinian poet, Mahmoud Darwish, translated by Munir Akash. He is also widely published on the worldwide web: The American Muslim, DeenPort, and his own website and poetry blog, among others: www.danielmoorepoetry.com, www.ecstaticxchange.wordpress.com. He is also currently poetry editor for *Seasons Journal,* and a new translation by Munir Akash of *State of Siege*, by Mahmoud Darwish, from Syracuse University Press. *The Ecstatic Exchange* Series is bringing out the extensive body of his works of poetry (a complete list of published works on page 2).

POETIC WORKS by Daniel Abdal-Hayy Moore
Published and Unpublished

Dawn Visions (published by City Lights, 1964)
Burnt Heart/Ode to the War Dead (published by City Lights, 1972)
This Body of Black Light Gone Through the Diamond (printed by Fred
    Stone, Cambridge, Mass, 1965)
On The Streets at Night Alone (1965?)
All Hail the Surgical Lamp (1967)
States of Amazement (1970)

Abdallah Jones and the Disappearing-Dust Caper (published by The
    Ecstatic Exchange/Crescent Series, 2006)
'Ala ud-Deen and the Magic Lamp
The Chronicles of Akhira (1981) (published by Zilzal Press with
    Typoglyphs by Karl Kempton, 1986, Sparrow on the
    Prophet's Tomb, 3 short books, The Ecstatic Exchange, 2009)
Mouloud (1984) (A Zilzal Press chapbook, 1995, Sparrow on the
    Prophet's Tomb, 3 short books, The Ecstatic Exchange, 2009)
Man is the Crown of Creation (1984)
The Look of the Lion (The Parabolas of Sight) (1984)
The Desert is the Only Way Out (completed 4/21/84) (Zilzal Press
    chapbook, 1985)
Atomic Dance (1984) (am here books, 1988)
Outlandish Tales (1984)
Awake as Never Before (12/26/84) (Zilzal Press chapbook, 1993)
Glorious Intervals (1/1/85) (Zilzal Press chapbook, ?)
Long Days on Earth/Book I (1/28 – 8/30/85)
Long Days on Earth/Book II (Hayy Ibn Yaqzan)
Long Days on Earth/Book III (1/22/86)
Long Days on Earth/Book IV (1986)
The Ramadan Sonnets (Long Days on Earth/Book V) (5/9 –
    6/11/86) (Published by Jusoor/City Lights Books, 1996)
    (Republished as Ramadan Sonnets by The Ecstatic Exchange,
    2005)
Long Days on Earth/Book VI (6-8/30/86)
Holograms (9/4/86 – 3/26/87)
History of the World (The Epic of Man's Survival) (4/7 – 6/18/87)

Exploratory Odes (6/25 – 10/18/87)
The Man at the End of the World (11/11 – 12/10/87)
The Perfect Orchestra (3/30 – 7/25/88)(Published by The Ecstatic Exchange, 2009)
Fed from Underground Springs (7/30 – 11/23/88)
Ideas of the Heart (11/27/88 – 5/5/89)
New Poems (scattered poems, out of series, from 3/24 – 8/9/89)
Facing Mecca (5/16 – 11/11/89)
A Maddening Disregard for the Passage of Time (11/17/89 – 5/20/90) (Published by The Ecstatic Exchange, 2009)
The Heart Falls in Love with Visions of Perfection (6/15/90 – 6/2/91)
Like When You Wave at a Train and the Train Hoots Back at You (Farid's Book) (6/11 – 7/26/91) (Published by The Ecstatic Exchange, 2008)
Orpheus Meets Morpheus (8/1/91 – 3/14/92)
The Puzzle (3/21/92 – 8/17/93)
The Greater Vehicle (10/17/93 – 4/30/94)
A Hundred Little 3-D Pictures (5/14/94 – 9/11/95)
The Angel Broadcast (9/29 – 12/17/95)
Mecca/Medina Time-Warp (12/19/95 – 1/6/96) (Published as a Zilzal Press chapbook, 1996, Sparrow on the Prophet's Tomb, 3 short books, The ecstatic Exchange, 2009))
Miracle Songs for the Millennium (1/20 – 10/16/96)
The Blind Beekeeper (11/15/96 – 5/30/97) (Published 2002 by Jusoor/Syracuse University Press)
Chants for the Beauty Feast (6/3 – 10/28/97)
You Open a Door and it's a Starry Night (10/29/97 – 5/23/98) (Published by The Ecstatic Exchange, 2009)
Salt Prayers (5/29 – 10/24/98) (Published by The Ecstatic Exchange, 2005)
Some (10/25/98 – 4/25/99)
Flight to Egypt (5/1 – 5/16/99)
I Imagine a Lion (5/21 – 11/15/99) (Published by The Ecstatic Exchange, 2006)
Millennial Prognostications (11/25/99 – 2/2/2000) (Published by the Ecstatic Exchange, 2009)
Shaking the Quicksilver Pool (2/4 – 10/8/2000) (Published by The Ecstatic Exchange, 2009)
Blood Songs (10/9/2000 – 4/3/2001)

The Music Space (4/10 – 9/16/2001) (Published by The Ecstatic Exchange, 2007)
Where Death Goes (9/20/2001 – 5/1/2002) (Published by The Ecstatic Exchange, 2009)
The Flame of Transformation Turns to Light (99 Ghazals Written in English) (5/14 – 8/21/2002) (Published by The Ecstatic Exchange, 2007)
Through Rose-Colored Glasses (7/22/2002 – 1/15/2003) (Published by The Ecstatic Exchange, 2007)
Psalms for the Broken-Hearted (1/22 – 5/25/2003) (Published by The Ecstatic Exchange, 2006)
Hoopoe's Argument (5/27 – 9/18/03)
Love is a Letter Burning in a High Wind (9/21 – 11/6/2003) (Published by The Ecstatic Exchange, 2006)
Laughing Buddha/Weeping Sufi (11/7/2003 – 1/10/2004) (Published by The Ecstatic Exchange, 2005)
Mars and Beyond (1/20 – 3/29/2004) (Published by The Ecstatic Exchange, 2005)
Underwater Galaxies (4/5 – 7/21/2004) (Published by The Ecstatic Exchange, 2007)
Cooked Oranges (7/23/2004 – 1/24/2005 (Published by The Ecstatic Exchange, 2007)
Holiday from the Perfect Crime (1/25 – 6/11/2005)
Stories Too Fiery to Sing Too Watery to Whisper (6/13 – 10/24/2005)
Coattails of the Saint (10/26/2005 – 5/10/2006) (Published by The Ecstatic Exchange, 2006)
In the Realm of Neither (5/14/2006 – 11/12/06) (Published by The Ecstatic Exchange, 2008)
Invention of the Wheel (11/13/06 – 6/10/07)
The Sound of Geese Over the House (6/15 – 11/4/07)
The Fire Eater's Lunchbreak (11/11/07 – 5/19/2008) (Published by The Ecstatic Exchange, 2008)
Sparks Off the Main Strike (5/24/2008 – 1/10/2009)
Stretched Out on Amethysts (1/13/2009 - 9/17/09)
The Throne Perpendicular to All that is Horizontal (9/18/09 -)

www.ingramcontent.com/pod-product-compliance
Lightning Source LLC
Chambersburg PA
CBHW032040150426
43194CB00006B/354